AF334068

OH AMERICA &
JANUARY 12TH, 1967

J. CHESTER JOHNSON

Grateful acknowledgement is made to the editors of *South and West* for permission to reprint the poems, "Darkness" and "The Big Sellout!".

The poem, "And Cherokee Sundown," was first published in *An American Sequence*, Copyright © 1969 by J. Chester Johnson.

First Printing: May, 1975
Printed and bound in the United States of America.

Juliet Press, 106 Willow Street, Brooklyn, New York 11201

Library of Congress Catalog Card Number: 75-12496

ISBN 0-914426-01-X

To D. A.

OH AMERICA

CONTENTS

DARKNESS

What light do you make on this tired earth?
Do you come from darkness deeper in yourself? And hunchback
and shackled drag darkness to the living? Do you tear
out someone else's darkness to hold it over them like a
hammer? Do you? Do you look for all that's hidden
or shy, because, in your own dark mind, all that's hidden from you
becomes your own terror?

Do I see you search out a stranger
for the night? But Oh! All the living is a stranger to
you. Hear the steps in the park behind you? Notice the
madman watching? What of your home: black draperies and cold tile?
And how's your wife: stiff and afraid of your loud stares?
And your children? Or do you have children? Strange to see you there,
proud and acting alone,

your children shaking like leaves. Yes we
know your darkness is your own weak mind. But what of light? Oh
yes, you have light, also, hidden in your shirt pocket
to work as a heart. You short-circuit the human race with a
bit of knowledge in a factory of darkness.
We know who came your way with a small thrill of fancy; now moths
are eating in her eyes,

she doesn't even care, she doesn't
even blow them away. What do you say? Darkness is best?
That we have to know darkness before light? Does the night
warm me? Do cold invisible hands love me? Does darkness glow
in any lover's excited face? Oh light is
what I enjoy! We knew light absolutely first, and we will
grow and grow more and more

1

violent and impatient to be
retaught in a clumsy night to follow darkness into
light. Yes we know freedom's light can also lead us to
darkness. Yes we know darkness is even older than sin and
at least twice as old as light. But we have only
recently come! And we came with dazzling fire in our lungs and
blinding love in our eyes!

Do not tell us about darkness, we
can't understand; oh yes, like the movie addict, we will
be teased and caught and convinced for a time. But then we
will disappear and retreat alone into an innocent
wilderness, and you will not hear us: we will be
carefully blowing and strengthening our flame. Later watchful
nights will reign, and you'll hear

infinitesimal whispers and
see a flicker over obscure mountains. But grinding out
like thunder, these will be done! Night will spread out with flames
and be just like day, light more real than darkness! Old men will be
glad and say it had to happen this way. . .And we'll
say to our children, "Do not destroy this light. Do not destroy
freedom, and don't scare it

away by demanding too much from
it, for freedom can also be darkness when it becomes
chaos. Watch out for those who control but don't love and
those who would steal your light to feed their darkness. But most of all,
give sanity and explanation to a world,
unmade, that magnificently tries to save itself again
with greater fears and snares."

AND CHEROKEE SUNDOWN

Prelude

5:00, thirty minutes before supper on Saturday afternoons, Virgil Trotter, Warren Stephenson, Al Williams, Ashton Stuckey, and I trudged home with our eyes covered in dirt and in the search for warm signs of Indians. A blade of grass shining just right on the sun was an arrowhead, a cold-charred fire surrounded by black rocks and doused with sand at the Twin Pines gravel pit was the last spot by the Cherokee scouts, and any roan colt dancing at one end of a rope in a backyard was bucking to get to Red Rock, the son of the chief. He was usually hiding in the shrubs for a quick getaway back to his tribe.

The Indians called it *The Cherokee Trail of Tears*. The army rode in wagons with Cherokees nudged close. No talking. Only when exiles fell or died. "It was spooky," one old man told my granddaddy, "the way they leaned over and died with faces like stones, the same looks put on statues."

When later the image of an ancient Cherokee returned to me, his Cherokee spirit was flowing, already blending with nature he'd saved like a gift.

And Cherokee Sundown

And Cherokee Sundown
      will wait out finally a dying man.
I'll be striped bass
and moon,
the crow and all of rain.
Sands will cover my blood.
I'll be howl
            and desert night.
The sand will color me with moon,
and I'll be the dew that's still in the fist.
I will be the touch
                  and a windfall.
Veins will untie me:
I travel a short distance only.

Oh the heavens break out,
Oh to scatter myself.
 The river is no longer wide,
how I cross it in a day
                  over the number of sons I have borne
and wives who stay,
you who carry my youth.

The sun that's with the crow
        knows me,   my name and my cause,
and hangs my distance on this hollow night
                  to the stars,
and the dust will catch me in the hills.
            Me,   this life,
I spin this life around me a vein,
and the vein's webbing holds me together.

           Oh I'll be
leaves tear into the wind!
           I am
too full of love I haven't time to free.
        The veins do wear out
this webbing that holds me only to this day.
I'll require you,   my sons,
                         my widows, to my death.
The sun will shade you more.
Do not lie
           silent into love.
                        Be strong.
                        Speak loudly.

No longer silent
into the hollow moon
                         to the last wind's
whistle and whining
days below the sky,
I hang my strength on the full moon
           on the path to the stars.
I catch the sky in the mountains,
and there the sun's very kind to old fighters —
           Sands will not ride me down,
I'm following *The Cherokee Trail of Tears.*

I've seen my past myself once over again now,
I'm not must wiser.
You who come to me through the dust
        and sun yourselves on my light and my death,
Follow the water and drink with an open fist,
           drink and swell smoothly,

                              Son of my last son,
                              Son of the pace. . .
That this calm,
I bless the days are past the feuds they made
Cherokee Sundown (youth dares me to meaning in the desert)
when days would feud with days
in the heroics of sundown.

Oh to scatter myself
    and fall from the hills with an echo
            and sun with the sun
and drink of myself as water,
a desert
        and spring,
first water in coming spring,
    ride with hedge and sageweed
and the scattered corn and dry seed.

NOTE FROM MONTICELLO

Prelude

After two years in New York City, Dickie Ann, my wife, and I decided to make ourselves a home in Monticello, a town of 6,000 in southeast Arkansas. My family had settled in the region 150 years before. There was another lure: 1969-70 was the year before full school desegregation, I taught in the black children's school, sixth through the twelfth grades. Because we always wait 'til the end to really try, it was my last chance to find people I had seen but I hadn't found.

The mayor was belched out of town in the grand ole tradition. There was a special election. Six white men, each one, we thought, beyond an energetically just age, entered the race. A consortium of reticent blacks and whites was spawned; and I was running for mayor. Ah, defeat is so bittersweet when you know you're right. At night, during the fun of the campaign, black men walked with me in their parcels of town. One night, Bobby Singer, who called himself "Breeches," and I appealed our way down a street I'd never explored. One house at the end was steadied on two-foot blocks and fairly large for those houses. A voice probed the dark, "Who is it?" "Breeches. And I want you to meet somebody."

The door opened into a room of two double beds and nothing else. A white man, about 65, gasped for more air in the older bed; he paid no attention to us. Gwendolyn Homer, one of the sixth graders, said, "We call him The Mixer." Then I first noticed the lighter wisp of her complexion. My imagination billowed; not until months later back in New York City did it settle down. I drew the old man as a father much younger and drew his son hating white blood that streamed through him; such hate ends in patricide. "Note From Monticello" is told by a white man who's a friend to the father.

Note From Monticello

You know, when we get real lonely, we seem
to think of people who were kind to us.
The mattress was shaggy and lumpy, and
he lay there vacuous and muttering
about the cold and religion. Some street
light leaked from huge cracks in the floor and walls.

I guess he knew the treat well (better than
anyone else I believed) how to live
out a hard story, but that alone they
were widely redemptive for each other's
strictures. The blacks were afraid he might kill
her one day or the whites would come and burn
up some of the will. Again, he looked near
death, shaking with washed-out splotches braggart
over his ashen body, blue toenails.

We waited on his part to be more than
he was, as you wait for your fears to turn
human, and they never do, or at least,
they stay more stern than you could expect them
to be: so rumors make it hard to like
someone until we know he has nothing
to do with the strike and bust of fiction.

He repeated the name, "Jacob," again
(the unknown has a name we recognize),
as if a colleague might then pull safe days
somewhere from the past, "Jacob!" And the wife
kept praying without holding caution straight,

as though she were rife with a long story
for an old friend, which resembled panic;
she didn't have any hope left, begging
the mechanic night wouldn't close with him.

His black friend and I, we'd awkwardly hear
and tell his stories. Some the way he told
them about the bristled, sear winter, and
in the sourness of summer dust had owned
his mouth, how he worked with no thumb after
he jammed a toned gin one September when
his hand got caught in metal works, the years
the crops failed and the family ate dough
by candlelight and the tears talked about
everything except food, and then machines
came. . .pickers that could do in a half-hour
what it took men's routines all day to do,
and there were no more mules, the hand plows leaned
against the barns, everybody moved to
town, the preened farmhouses broke down a board
at a time until they were all used up
for firewood, then money came in the mail
for the tasteless gup of doing nothing —
Bill said he didn't like that 'cause children
never learned the people money came from.

The daughter sat crystalline on the floor
across the room with her lover and hummed
so indifferently she was freeless.
Bravely unplumbed, she thought she was pregnant,

she wasn't sure: it meant little amid
the incautious scene but to her prudence.
She was fussily hid, wondering how
dark her baby would be and the color
of its eyes. She was sixteen and acid
impatience; the visitor life did seem
pretty long 'til she could have a baby.

Younger children, several set almost
as wan as Bill, three as dark as others
on the street, knocked around in the next room,
feeling the dead mood through the wall, playing
wild so the tomb wouldn't be felt. They had
already learned on the street, as Bill said,
"If your care grows away from laughter, your
body instead gives relief from worry."

The last winter rain kept crushing the day;
and voices could be heard quickened to shacks.
The winds still lay in open fields that night
and didn't quite make it to town, a slow
town even for southeast Arkansas, where
the land would know to rise. Just a very
hard rain outside, and blithe girls running home;
heavy shoes crunching in the wet gravel;
nobody much to roam the diversion.
It seemed everybody sensed that something
unusual was happening, and so
rumors were clinging cold to the houses:
a few reports had him dead already

(we'll rush people toward divinity
in order that we become more divine),
others had him a turn for the better.
I guess it's like that on the way to death:
people find the commoner of dying
too easy to understand, they make truth
alittle more confusing on their own.
He had found many sleuth friends on the street;
he didn't have many friends through our town.
Most whites wondered how he could live as blacks
lived on that hand-me-down street just beyond
the breathing sewage ditch. Other wnites had
it as bad, worse even, but he had been
an exception. Story-clad blacks wondered
why whites let him live noiselessly. Yes, it's
true, a suspicious man doesn't have friends.

Envy admits that love was a stranger
appetite with them, that she was older
than most and didn't care much about men
before him; slowly astir, he wasn't
interested in one or any more
until they had started one fall picking
the season's crops. Love would pour a secret
for them, who didn't talk to anyone
else down a row and bent for taking fruit
or vegetables. Like a gun erupting,
occasionally his father's other
voice would shatter through rows, "You leave the black
woman alone, or for her, there will be

nothing left of you." Still one afternoon,
as everyone left the fields and started
home along the jejune and dirt-dusty
road, Bill and Lucy walked off together.
Next morning they strolled into ready rows
with something steadier that might be risk.
He carried their lunch in a sugar sack.
History has it that sometime after,
they moved further back into the country
roads and went to town then only to sell
tomatoes at an auction. It's told that
his father pell-mell almost killed him on
a couple of nights 'cause of his Lucy,
but that was a long time ago during
planting, and no one really remembers.

"The bother don't sting so bad," he would say
to her some mornings (which discovered there
was enough creation that day to serve
all creation), as they tried the calm, long
roads. "Hell, it ain't so good either, but while
the crops hold out strong, we can keep ourselves."

They called him The Mixer, especially
as babies started to come in bunches
with their skin to be a sweet, meak color
of tan and hair that was kinky enough
but worn heavy and straight. It seemed babies
came faster, after rough machines wouldn't
quit and then Bill and Lucy left the fields.

They called him The Mixer when Lucy went
to apply for the yields from welfare. They
called him The Mixer on the sleeping street.

Slapping over the tin roof, a downpour
of rain will eat greedily on a house.
It was as though birth signs came here again
for the end and earth's elements washed him
again. Between specimen, thick mumblings
and the low calling of old and new names,
a very tired question, mindlessly sound,
would stand like claims, "Is that rain? Is that rain?"

His dying dreams I could well imagine:
a worker standing before his work, hands
outstretched sibylline to the horizon;
plants now dripping of mildew at daybreak
and his arms then breaking with that first sweat;
miracle fingers will awake, moving
faster than time down a row — that harvest
rhythm that is a habit forever;
beautiful, atwist fruit all in a pile,
or giant sacks of wistful cotton caught
in a wagon, as the sun's going down
and everything thought glows either yellow
or orange; stiff mules are steaming power
under his grip, and reins snap against hide
as a man and a mule concur to first
open up the ground; his arms once more felt
like woven wire with each sovereign muscle

cut to its svelte self throbbing from pleasure
of work; and smelling of the mule and sweat
and fertilizer, he would sit before
a meal of dry threat, meat, tomatoes, brown
syrup, and biscuits; and the consumptive
odor of fish that drown frying reminds
him of the fugitive catch; and grateful,
all the women in the fields watch closely,
as he sheds his shirt and hardens his back
alittle, as he turns around seeing
women see him; dirt crumbles in his hand,
sifts through enormous fingers — he shuffles
it gently and simply in drunken palms;
the tiny ten acre farm he'd rather
owned. These must have been his best dreams passing
forever further from what's remembered.

Everyone here, also those feeling here
feeling this death, did not even whisper
now, but thought of cavalier stories that
everybody thought were true. It was odd
about Bill: nobody told much after
being with him, and, God knows, nobody
caught him doing much, but few people could
doubt tales about him. He was a coward
and understood "white trash" to lots of whites
but mean as snakes with no mercy to as
many blacks. One place it could be told he,
more than once, has just refused to fight, and
yet another spot he'd torn the bare throats

from several grown men. Both were believed,
for fame notes that a man's reputation
depends on the people who will hear it —
the dominions they like and the talents
they're afraid of and admit to. Seldom
did the political stories prove true,
but after the winning voices stopped, it
didn't matter through the daze: he'd become
the stories about him, and some women
laughed at him, and others hid their children.

The five of us sat akin listening
to him breathe and struggle with his unshaped
words or names. We knew he was alone then
while we escaped death on the floor and so
pretended chance formed a destined purpose.
The woman, who bore his children and he
loved, no longer prayed for us, but with her
head between her knees, she wouldn't be seen.
The daughter, hands locked to a lover's, had
her hope careen off blunt effects; the face
she chose didn't want to show care, but firmed
at courage that laid dully with her head
on a mistermed, separate, benign chest.

A black man, the only real friend, leaned close
to my mind. From next door, he'd dreamed with Bill
of other, gibbose times: when the weather
was good, how they could smell the land. This man
felt he was lucky — he had a job (at

the funeral van driving funerals,
but he had a job). "I wish I could work
regular like you too," Bill would say now
and then on rich, quirk evenings when they would
talk just to be together. And then there
was me, white, like quintessence of silver,
on the oldest share of the floor, mourning
his coming death. If I hadn't changed so
and this town hadn't changed, I couldn't be
here now. I realize the show as well
as cost of it, and I am ashamed by
it, that what I love is only what I
learn to love and I am allowed to love.

We really met the first time when I got
back home, going on ten more years ago.
A stout man, blot-balding too much for my
early twenties, I had heard of Bill, but
there was no reason to appreciate
him; and then one uncut afternoon, I
took a wrong street where he was digging out
the ditch that passed his house. I saw a friend,
but Bill searched about my unskilled style; I
guess I began to love his liking me.

A common horse philosophy tempted
me best: not newly abstract or gutless,
surely nothing to be taught in school, just
a very hard will to live with what you
like, what you must dislike didn't matter.

He shared his tough mind, and when I would find
myself believing him too much, life would
seem too easy. He inclined me to think,
more than once, it was people who confused
life, which was really pretty simple. I
wondered how a used man right from the fields
could think as he could. He only had time
was his reply, with his crops gone and no
jobs or rhyme around and with his woman
and the welfare wanting only more kids.

He was, as alot of grand people said,
like a disease (not the bid's cruel way
they meant): you just became more like him and
didn't try to see yourself the way you
had before, all firsthand, ever again.

It seemed he lost his head for a couple
of things: he'd talk about the constant change
of supple seasons, as though it were now
to spell the last time he'd spot redemption,
and for his eyes it was, I guess. "Every
winter will run at sort of a certain
plowing — and comes different and treats land
different. Now listen, after one goes,
habits don't stand up the same." Maybe he
had guessed right, though I kinda doubted if
anyone ever noticed. The other
was his stiff craving for good food — he'd say
he'd walk a long morning for a fine meal.

Only this morn I wandered their kitchen,
grousing shelves could appeal to his small laugh.

Precious things come only in small amounts
and are not often in a man's life: he
sits and counts patiently for them, but if
too patiently, they never come, and if
too impatiently, they are missed. Among
contradictions, it's just a whiff of luck.
They had loved each other, he knew that well:
he loving her abit more probably,
though he'd never tell it — you could receive
for his recollections something willed more
tender than hers, whose at times were flat or
bored or tired. A long time 'fore he mentioned
Lucy, then all at once, from such plucked, ripe
satisfaction. I was privileged, I
knew that too well. Just a swipe by my quick
curiosity in fame could persuade
me to search him further for frank blessings
until he conveyed the friend that he was?

Theirs was a love that got better with time.
It had so gradually grown steady
and new the longer they would mime and were
denied. A great deal of living slowly
together and not many fights. It was
the toughness, that's what clarity had taught:
the hard times with few friends and little work
and sometimes no jobs, cold nights with no glad

electricity and no perk wood to
burn out the frost, or blistering under
the tin that held all the sun, or the land
was gone forever, or the offended
garden wouldn't grow anymore. It was
hard being together alone with bland-
asking children and the gnats-buzz measure
nature barely gave. There, that out of hard
times came a strong love. For him, it made him
stronger. Barred, I didn't know about her.

I felt the carelessness as the first son
came home. Springtime again, it'll be two
years since he left the skeleton temper
of Chicago. I was fixed when he threw
his duffel bag into the quiet room
and waited to hear overdue pleasure
from someone. A sister cried and spun her
scrawny arms around his neck, and Lucy,
gently preserving amateur thoughts, kissed
and hugged him. He shook his father's baited
hand and mine quickly, and went away. It
was the late inflated summer before
I saw him again. He pretended there
had been no modest chance for us to meet.

"Explanation can wear no excuse," Bill
swore, and swallowed the large reason his son
wanted home. But like all secrets, of course,
the secret was the one that finally

told. First time in anger, Bill grouched the rare
scamp should probably still be in jail. And
then once, a fair face, hurt by confusion,
he wondered why anyone cared to burn
down a store and what were Jews anyway.

The taciturn son had been the favored
child, Bill expected, and I saw he could
be arrogant: careless comparisons
he made; and stood mean with his laughs, he smiled
when we didn't like him. The blunt tartness
was blamed on a plan that decorated
him noblesse, the easiest skin among
the children; for while he was in school, he
pranced 'round like any peacock showing its
colors, arranging parody with such
sweet taunt, and next bragged on the gifts of white
freedom. If the moral's true, it's that pride's
disloyal: lying bright on a neighbor's
front steps to await attention for his
difference, he was congratulating
himself once on the quiz that infects meet
response to quiet his flat gall, "Black men
will always drink the worst of these places.
The suffering has often been deadly
tolerance, and there's no proof you've ever
suffered for any cause. What's the result
or greater award? A more convenient
suffering? Every compromise has your
weakness and supports the certainty of

your next impure defeat. You've been waiting
around here all your life for a white man
to do something for you. You don't even
get a crumb of a veteran corn stick.
White men help white men, and that's it. Black men
help black men. An exit is the relief
you have. Again freedom's the only way
to stop pain, freedom rejects history.
Now take the excellence of the cities,
like Chicago. We're freely building there
a black man's country — black stores, black cafes,
black night clubs, black banks, through black money. And
the motive stays black or blame will kill us."
A bald oak reminded me of thoughts that
occur in winter, and his arch voice no
longer assumed me at its tired leisure.
I tasted another emotion, but
I couldn't finish its size; embarrassed,
alittle gut-scared, alittle crazy
even, I knew in a way the promise
he meant: I didn't belong there is what
he could not dismiss, and if I didn't
belong there, yes, Bill didn't belong there.

Rain was withering, more sounds were trying
the weather; elsewhere Bill had stopped even
muttering. How damn easy it is to
die (and I reached up to test his strength), you
make noise and fight all through your life, and then
always die like any beggar. She turned

on him, she turned on him, buying a son's
grief and sojourned predictions he made; and
everything he hated she suspected
hated him. Bill didn't think the words would
ever end rejected. "She sure missed him
alot, more 'an I knew," he'd say without
a wrinkle to a lip. "She chose always
to favor about him, to build special
confines for his beliefs, always helped him
more than the others — maybe 'cause he was
the first gem, a boy, or for something else."

Just a sparkle (they droned when they called me),
a blade popped open in the sun, and death
shimmered and struck: (Sanctity drained through each
violent crack.) Bill knelt unfree into
the sidewalk and held a torn side; the son
running to a few railroad tracks caught last
glimpses of a dreaded father beside
the bus station, with Lucy standing like
a wife of twenty-three, undried years. We
lifted Bill with fear and left his blood spot
for the stories. We carried him the three
blocks home — a white-hot stranger, the better
friend and me. I knew everything to know
without asking: the bus for Chicago
passed rather low and everyone stared; Bill's
wife, deserted, fiddled two tickets; I
suppose Bill strained to keep her from going.

I considered his sigh way that always
worked the same and his rough house which doubled
everyone's honesty, as rain peppered
the tin. The bubbled children hit the wall
again: where could they go, and who'd they go
to, what would they know about yesterday?
The black friend slow-crawled angrily to weak
feet, looked into the closed features, which now
remained of Bill: "But this matters — Bill'll
come back. How tomorrow he'll bring the mail
and collect the rent, sell me bad whiskey
and try to buy my daughters. He'll cuss me
and call me anything he wants to and
break my heart and break my back. All the sure
signs of pain must hide our Bill once again.
Someday, we'll see obscure Bill tho, prissin'
down the street, waving to everybody
and asking how the morning is, letting
our children go by. Luckily open,
everybody'll wave back and tell him
the morning's just fine and we're gonna get
even better without a whim. Yes, I
see him coming right up to me, and we'll
sit upon the porch and talk as we used
to. Far down the road, he'll steal some laughing
now. Great God, I see him laughing now. Pain,
like an oak, does not grow to the sky." I
breathed richly on soft rain at the screen door,
but the chill of death rattled me. Soon land
would blossom out all over again, and

men feel his sun and eat blueberries in
his fertile shade. Someone else might have shone
on his Lucy. He'll be gone! He'll be gone.

THE BIG SELLOUT!

Prelude

If someone is free, we absorb the life. It may free us, it may be rejected, or we may assume it's just another ego excess. But it may whip us in the face, hurting us like hell, because we finally have to admit that, at least this time, courage is finally just courage. Alexander Solzhenitsyn. We then set him apart, and he's responsible for the truth for which we're not. That's the way I chewed at myself after Solzhenitsyn of the Soviet Union was awarded the Nobel Prize for Literature, and his life was given an exclamation point: the years in a labor camp for a phrase against Stalin; his triumphant speech before the Writers' Union, which had censored and expelled him; the years cancer wrecked his body to be arrested finally in the darkest pit of him. I wrote "The Big Sellout!" in honor of Solzhenitsyn and the day the Nobel Prize exposed his peculiar freedom and the assorted crimes of Soviet oppression. Alexander Solzhenitsyn was employed as a math teacher when *One Day in the Life of Ivan Denisovich* first appeared in print. Shukhov had the eyes we saw through. *Iunost* is a Russian literary magazine. This poem was published in Poland in the spring of 1971.

The Big Sellout!

written in commemoration of the day, October 8, 1970

It was the same feeling you get when an old friend you thought might
have died

comes to your front door.
It was that kind of joy, wasn't it? Surprise Joy?
And told by telephone made it more magical. . .
No humans, just words. And sudden feelings.
It was like a religious experience for those who are religious.
Tonight, they sent you the news, Alexander Solzhenitsyn.
You won.
But while you're winning, your country's falling apart;
so you must be sacrificed.
Didn't you know that in this cold war
no man can win in his own right, but must win for his country?
And it's automatic, the more rights his country wins around this world
the less he has.
In this time of nations, only nations can actually win.

I hear it's cold over there,
and the wind can be as sour as walnuts.
We don't know your country very well,
though, it seems, as far back as I can remember,
we've judged our country by what your country did.
I remember one warming afternoon a long time ago,
discussing justice with a friend:
I said America couldn't really be bad
as long as there was Communist Russia.
I don't believe that's all true anymore.

The night is too cold even for dogs there.
And icicles weigh pounds hanging on faint street lamps.

Everywhere cruel sounds of a coming oppressive winter.
Your name is spoken very low like a bribe.
Your words are hardly uttered,
and the children who stir by the fire don't even know who you are.
Papers don't mention you.
No radio station carries your name.
You might as well be a math teacher in some small town outside of Moscow,
or worse, you might as well be dead, Alexander Solzhenitsyn!

Solzhenitsyn (the name sort of tingles in my throat),
who has loved you so much
that you could love your country so much that seems to hate you?
You've grown a longer beard since you were Shukhov,
the long whiskers tell a grim story.
And your eyes warn of a cold bitter season just ahead.

I sit in a desk chair by a window and look over small parts of a city,
thinking terribly abstract thoughts,
while art dies in my country and artists are being killed in yours.
Yes, it's old but true, we get what we do and don't do.

I read *IUNOST* like a child,
looking at the color pictures
and wishing I could understand the words.
But the pictures tell me, Alexander Solzhenitsyn, you're in trouble:
Russian soldiers celebrate on government steps,
and all the poets wear uniforms beside their poems.

This was the day Russia's conscience was examined!
It's a bad report. She has trouble in her judgment.

And when she turns against her own, her true face shows cruel
and barbarous to a world that waits instantly for an answer.
Russia, will you lose in the morning scared of your own art's shadow?
And your strongest and most tender children
will quiver with bitterness at that moment against you.
What children, Oh what children, can you love, Great Government?
those that say you are beautiful without looking,
those that speak while reading speeches,
those that shout without thinking,
those that have no pity because they're pitiful?
Are those the voices that make proud Russia?
Those voices out of tired minds!
Who tells you who you are?
Who tells you
who cries or dies alone shivering in a burned out alley filled with snow,
what your people say when they walk at night together,
or where you must go to cure yourself?

So you sold out, Solzhenitsyn!
you'd rather be truthful than sorry.
So you told your country what time it was,
and what the letters on public buildings meant,
and that prisoners were almost painless,
hungry as wolves with frozen beards,
and children disappeared in the dead of winter,
and women cried for them all right.
So you sold out your country for the truth!
Who was interested anyway?
So we care and sob at the deaths of people we don't even know
and choke on somebody else's hunger
and shiver when someone else is buried in snow.
So who cares anyway, Solzhenitsyn? You big sellout!

Where was your exile? In the outer reaches of your country's conscience?
Better than death maybe?
Ideas just disappear in this country too,
not by fear so much, mostly by neglect.
God! To see the faces of pudgy men glow in fury at your injustice,
but with red damp cheeks, they take off their coats
and brush away the cold by rubbing themselves brutally;
in a pub they ask for a drink, sit down, and talk about work.
Where are you tonight, Solzhenitsyn?
In your home waiting for the darkening silence to be defined into some
                                        dark action?
Who understands you pain?
Who holds your thoughts secure now and your body to forget its dead
                                        cancer?
Who believes you're a marked mind?
Tonight, houses of Russia are dimmer because of you, Alexander
                                Solzhenitsyn:
Some in tribute! Others sink from your hard vision!
What prison can hide?
What meetings have you called for tomorrow? Oh, the Whole World's
                                Watching!

What you've known and imagined and what Russia imagines you to be
create your art.
The pressure in your blood!
Who felt it strongest last? You, pulsing like a mad flood,
or those you attacked with it?
Your conscience is everywhere!
        truth with pity!
                a mind recording precisely the suffering and disbelief!
                        fascinated by experience!

You need the best of friends, Solzhenitsyn,
who warn you when it's not safe out,
and you can lie still and positive
in the deepest closet of your mind.
They'd pass notes in the night,
bringing to you and taking away your only freedom: of the mind and
                                                        imagination!

What are those notes of yours anyway?
Just stories about what simple humanity wants to but can't do?
Is that all? Weather reports on your country!
A disgusting temper that wants to tell when it's all cold inside
and a hot stove should be raging.
Yes your kind always get hurt;
you're the ones who won't take no for an answer:
you want to know why men hurt,
but you're not told. . .it's only "NO" to the question!
Don't you see, Alexander Solzhenitsyn, that when you ask serious
                                                        questions,
you're unhappy, and what government can stand unhappiness for its
                                                        people?

Who are you to let everyone look at great Russia with sorry glares?
You with no dreams!
Where's that eye for the future?
There in your conceit tying up the present with the past,
reducing the glory of millennium!
Who would sell out his man for pieces of paper but a traitor!

If you have felt cruelty come in a frown
                    and orders without reasons,

you feel with Solzhenitsyn in a quietly lighted room tonight,
all alone with his thoughts,
the terror of power. . .
and who has felt these can imagine
that somewhere men with sweaty hands and disciplined laughs
will decide in gaudy lights and marble floors
what to do with one man who sits alone.
This man is that part of each of us
which stands aside from the rest
and is our courage forever!

JANUARY 12TH, 1967

Prelude

Wherever fantasies have been concocted, people act illusory. And yet whenever behavior behaves desperately, we simply do not know the protagonists. He knew them a short time; however, the moments since have sharpened the recognition.

It's hard to be from a small, Southern town these days, but danger doesn't stop you if freedom is still a chance. If not, it's probably best you stay home.

He discovered why boys don't sacrifice ignorance easily: they think they sacrifice innocence. But they're not innocent until they cancel the reasons they are ignorant. That may be hard to understand, but if you've ever believed in anything more beautiful than your own creations, you know the laws you must violate.

The facts about him? Nineteen, more likely. No father. A good mother. His brother much like him. An athlete, he'd almost forgotten his body taught pure lessons. The country's image changed fast, while the people he had trusted were slowly angered by change.

Although he drifted away from a hometown for awhile and, as he saw it again, he saw it differently doesn't mean he then cared any less for it. But some people always interpret questions to mean exclusion. Anyway, when love's not returned, you can't force it, or it becomes a lie; and there's only one alternative, and that's to love something else.

A town and innocence were no longer the same, and the City waited like a stranger you'd rather pass.

As a rule, courage is staying sane in the face of no escape.

January 12th, 1967

And my brother had said once, "A city is land
Disturbed, full of danger and cockroaches." For pride,
The highway's too busy with cattle trucks, tankers,
Limousines, jitneys, cycles over eight lanes of
Asphalt; the whole world smells like gasoline. Heated
Fumes smother us while the bad winter advances;
And car heaters blast out the idylls. Cattle trucks
Convince cautious beasts; tankers tame oil; jitneys haul
Tired workers; limousines carry a rare kind of
Man-giant, so it seems; and, as the remaining
Generality, minimized cars piously
Collect the other people back to the City.

We're all in a gas and smoke, manmade, but the haze
Separates us. Still we're bumper to bumper; our
Almost outrageous bodies next to bodies and
Hard as hell do follow the strongest bluff once more.
Refineries can stand starkly white as well as
Unapproachable: they stand like gods along the
Highway; then fences three times as tall as I am
Restrict factories and airports. Looking far off
To hills, I distinguish only features that are
Arrogantly before me: a fruit truck shaking;
Tankers ordering all liquid; amid the acts
Of greatness, whole families who can live or die
Today in a Volkswagen demand the City.

The quiet muscle that joins my back and neck now
Twitches for renewal: I've gone 1200 miles
Without sleep! In America is sleep at all

So unimportant: the rule might be our strength yet;
Then I'm unsure of a pride that lasts so long: a
Challenge I never saw and winning I never
Wanted. News broadcasts can't help my head, but I tune
Every clarity to dissolve sleepiness; my
Eyes ready to black out with aim, my body's much
Too heavy, and I stick hard to a brash, plastic
Seat cover. At home, Mother, with a laugh hanging
Out on the words, would have said, "You look just like death
Warmed over again." One foot's immovable on
The accelerator, and it's been hours since
My last meal. For sake of suggestion, my stomach
Once wrinkles too loudly, it can't wait much longer.

Even if I do not want them, friends'll defer
And ask each other when I'll arrive, but friends so
Immediate to the City aren't friends at all.
To wander is to excite an American,
So that minor thoughts of lonely perception will
Absolve me. Redeemed by contradictions, maybe
I'm inspired by somebody else's loneliness?

I bought Little Car to roam: slick, white, red and quite
Upholstered, a good immunity to classic
Myopia. Mostly I've tried freedom for short
Trips and abortive long ones: I always find a
Sinless cause to go home; there are always better
Reasons to endure than to simply complete a
Correction, than to see this country, to ingest
Its feelings and devote myself to it, to love

It better by spending my youth with it. Anger
Makes every celebration of rejection much
Easier; however, capital decisions
Never last very long: that's wrong and I know it.

But here I am, sleepy, cold, alittle bitter
With horns blaring, metal grinding. Motors expand.
People are daft, cussing and carefully mean. Grand
Queues of impatient traffic — I don't know them, I
Didn't witness people and machines mingle in
Theoretical compatibility and
Sensual enlightenment: I never saw these
People explain themselves one day into years in
Inorganic choices all humans constitute.

Cars wrecked in the shoulders are wheelless cars, rusted
Axiles. For warped, bent and cut hoods, someone drove faith
Nowhere. Two automobiles, junked carcasses, are
Believed for leaning on each other; imagine
New machines on a great venture will someday be
Hanging stripped and corroded in fluency! The
Prospect is inevitable, and the effect
Zealotry: quicker than metal works and healthy
Men too, pity will change to mediocrity.
Although a tale can only have one ending, the
Proposition everything will at last be ruined
Dedicates the human to novel suicide.

Magnetized to New York, objects edge more for space.
Posters are no sense. We jam our brakes and expect

To escape, swiping property at every chance.
I'm honking like I'm crazy: if I drove this way
In Arkansas, I would surely be arrested
Any second. A restless truck jerks on my side,
And I blow it out of the path with my horn. The
Pressure of fatigue can cancel a selective
Courage; and it's not sequential to want something
As much as I do, and solving the desire, to
Be as undeveloped as I am! Out of dull
Progress, not alone in pathological noise,
I would wish to wander home sure, Madisonville
Of a progressive afternoon with neither rough
Edges as motives nor solemnity as peace.

To fail a view I radicalized! But I can't,
Magnifying the country and verifying
So much of its history against its future,
Live from hand to mouth. If I should turn decisions
Around to face envy, people who don't even
Know reasons I try would know I greedily failed.

And somewhere in the midst of their alternative,
The City's mind, Victor and Mary-Helen are
Straining for their ideas to work; as stubborn,
Southern expatriots, they will, of course, want to
Know the prophetic times and places, and will laze
Over each word I tell them. They worry about
Madisonville like people who would wish for bane
From their bonds: they remember in laughs old hardness
And say the imprimatur was unfair, agree

How they did embarrass the town or how it would
Embarrass them; Madisonville's still adding to
Their quaint recesses of sad legends. Anyway,
It will spoil you once, and you never recover.

A station's dented sign shall recognize fading
Power: I waste mysterious and constricting
Gasoline by jabbing at people and at their
Collective ambition. Worthless metal scraps and
Chunks of glass gravel the driveway. Pumps smeared with oil.
From a grotesque flit of a shave, eyes of a gas
Pumper are bloodshot-straight for me; breath imbues me
With cigars and antiseptic; a gor-bellied
Swell overhangs his belt, but it's a spot to stuff
A towel; his hands are heavy and savage; and, as
He clears the windshield, rubber that has sewn such close
Glass crackles. "Today's a burner," and he smiles at
A reward of silence; "the way they're showing out,
Something's gonna climb on those bastards." A towel's
Also available for anger. "You know who.
Never for a Goddamn thing, they'll lie around. And
The government excuses them. But that's over
If they keep this perversity. Let 'em riot,
Get everybody mad enough." Satisfaction
Runs so deep he isn't vulnerable; hate is
Out on his body, and the surety he once
Reconciled returns as a theme to hurt frailty.
He'd tear into me if I gave him the angle.

There is no election to a riot; for one

Excellent act completes any necessary
Reaction; and injury stops the procedure
Of ultimatums. The aptitude of cities
Is burning, the blocks I pass are an evidence
To some failure, and the purpose of scars says
That there is never an objective solution
To suffering. I could have seen an innocent
Negotiator who dies in the street scream for
A recovery of the last chance. Would I hope
Reality has diminished into a mere
Likelihood? The accelerator's tougher or
I'm weaker. All directions appear to conclude
In the same place; so I drive down the nearest street,
Follow the uncertain instinct that I fully
Discover the suspension of options, and yet
Feel I am blindly leading myself the right way.

The City confines my better purpose; thus I
Shake my head to save my eyes from the heavy weight
Of no sleep: oppression would neutralize courage.
The performance of the City is much more than
Familiar while indefinite: for among
Suffocation, dense pines persuade over me at
The first walk through the timber, swollen gray in the
Cold that can echo to a distant sound rattling
Over the unmuffled ground. Voices and warnings
Caught in walled streets, homes are stacked on homes, trucks also
Wrenched, growling drivers well-tried between freedom and
Containment. And the grinding of garbage. And all
The sirens, motors and horns. And thick heights that are

Part of darkness terrorize me! Thoughts, my logic,
My recourse contract! Into the popular guts
Of the City! I'm detached from persuasion and
Recall: not seeing people, but fearing numbers
Of them; not even presuming architecture,
But another flat, blank structure; although drama
Would want to speak, I console myself with caution.

A flabby man sweating briefly through a sweat-browned
Undershirt inside some dirty window, boys with
Hair riding long and gay, foreign languages on
A corner when shouts discount the words and thoughts; then
Artificial lights borrow alittle day with
The sun lost between buildings: darkness does not live
Well in the City where pain will go where there is
No shine here. Girls wait alone, executives wave
Fast for a taxi to take them away, couples
Glare off and talk into themselves. While I could drive
Forever eastward on a crosstown channel, long
Distance amplifies sirens once southern in the
Island: a cold, demented plan rising further
Into a louder, nearer, more desperate mind!
Sirens yelling, screaming revenge; they're raging for
Protection! Four police cars cry through me and swerve
Pieces of traffic, and my perception follows
As far as it can. Red Flashes blinking out of
Sight. Police head north somewhere I've never been and
Only a bad curiosity would ever
Take me: I die daring so much variety.

What will cause a riot will sponsor slightly more
Than when people don't get protection they want, they'll
Riot. Anticipating aversion erupts
Into aversion? If having a certain thought
When no one listens but people say lessons that
Are always said, do you jerk and order someone
To listen to you? Who are the rioters now
If they resist the same results but will destroy
The same facades? So when they're different for the
Reasons they fight, then the reasons they must fight are
Located in the animal they're fighting. Where
Without warning nothing's again in control, quips
Rape without worry and steal, shoot down without a
Conscience the conclusions of a street, quietly
Bomb without forgiving the ambivalence that
Exploded. After all's burned and everyone's killed
Lust thinks should be then, the people left are still each
Other's one more final resolution. Waiting
For splendid change? It poorly flares! Firebombers will
Be guileless firebombers, priests only honest priests!

Gardens with new hedgerows and old flowers can split
An avenue, and shops barely comfortable
In small spaces thinly run along major streets.
Manikins hang naked, awkwardly permanent.
Wide streets, too well kept: manicured promenades look
Manicured; but wrought-iron fences whisked with carved
Work are handsome as well as easy. I distrust
An uncomfortable man who will play servant
To smile at a tough wife for a tip. Another
Inefficient beggar drunk in a corner leans

To ask for a passing nickel and falls into
His hole to sleep the dust off his mind some more. A
Long notion remains so normal it's vague: here a
City is a panorama of omissions.

Simply claimed by possessive, impervious streets,
Pitiless streets, I gaze at symbols becoming
More human, which yet regard solitude as a
Generalized weakness; I resemble more of
Specter, the solemn foreigner hired to fully
Evaluate indigenous appetites. Eyes
Dilating in sunlight, a distended nerve, and
No sleep; fingers meakly twitch whenever I think
Of ambience of the night. And tamely, because
Inevitability of an answer rests
Within perfection of choices, I'll knock on the
Generous door and affectionately delay
Victor and Mary-Helen; and they'll happily
Suspect and confirm it's really me; and I will
Emboss us on brief history, not as if they
Were separate from conditions I represent.
It's better three people enjoy themselves, not just
Each other. We've had bad times, often for the more
Excellent and ironic fun of them. And for
Our natural disrespect, jealousy has hurt
Us; but different places deal different times.

Such neon testimony! 24-hour
Parking! A flagellated Little Car. Cities
Weren't contemplated for cars — that's the truth —, and a

Curb jutting a stoical tire bumps my cubic
Dizziness. The lot is empty, but a lazy
Dog chews a hat by a disabled fence. No one
Here? I switch off the motor; independently
Little Car snatches and stalls. The details of the
Trip are deposited amid the machine; with
Money the only necessity before sleep
And revenge, with every other particular
Familiarity abandoned, I follow
The invitation of the City. Vacant to
The idea of direction or revision,
I feel the chill of not knowing attack my neck.
Victor had lectured, "No, it's easiest to first
Call from Grand Central." The street conforms to the last
Remnants of exhaustion with emptily displayed
Boxes famous in crashed-out windows, tart garbage
Falling over gutters. Sounds are solitary,
Almost mean, but I expect every quiet noise
As it snaps. The sun sneaks out of walls or over
Pious buildings; even descended, systems blast!

By constant shags of wood and cracks of brick, I do
Recover to the warm fragility of a
Bar, where prehistoric creaks invaded minor
Pleasures and pity derived from ages of the
Flesh and fierce style; the caustic odor of cloth-rot
Is too human. Is destruction always resolved
In weaker elements? Machinists forever
Unraveling the day's varied suspicions, which
Would limit a worker's production, increase the

Value of a joke by increasing the noise. I
Ask the peripatetic bartender for a
Phone directory; however, Victor's escaped
The synopsis! So I lapse, order a beer, and
Blend. Workers mumble another site: how they do
Or don't do their jobs; rivets are being misplaced,
And drilling's off schedule; lines followed perfectly
Are veterans' portion; new men just fucking things
Up princely perform as though they'd never seen a
Good piece of equipment. A few years, nothing will
Ever get built. Grease rests like an ancient spot on
A moodless cheek as a spent worker then amply
Exercises his right to hate yet another
Subject: what's happening there? how many police,
Firemen or thugs have been injured? A small fellow
With husk for a voice doesn't dread temper and blurts,
"It should be cleaned. Take 'em out and not let 'em back
Until they're checked. Police'd know who to arrest
Next time." One drunk, no longer sunk deep in his sleep,
Sways on an uncertain balance and whispers, "Is
That kinda stupid? To kill a dog to get at
His fleas?" A special stranger, satisfied in his
Exile and elevation, then machinates with
An ancient outrage: "Shut up, old son of a bitch,
What do you know? You ain't got no sense. Go back and
Suck your bottle." Talk wanders off like a stray child.

"How can I get to Grand Central?" So I invoke
Privity with a muscle-faced black man sitting
Supply beside me. Mostly a smirk confines a

Resistance, although he must perfectly spin a
Perfectly new quarter. "Just up the Avenue."
"How far?" "42nd Street." Coarse and pointed, he
Still includes more than I think he will: "Stay on the
Bowery 'til it's Third Avenue. Straight 'til you
Hit 42nd Street. Then ask someone." "Can I
Walk all the way there?" "God, yes." Extra words rub hard
On disregard; and he turns slowly there to wind
Tension and penetrates a cold, carved stare into
The pit of my naiveté; somewhere I quiver
From his hate, which is now inside of me staring
Back out at him. Resolved in an independent
Indolence, I stop the experiment; for the
Definition of a mere bluff is the only
Reward of a successful confrontation. How
Easy it is to hate someone when you do not
Know if he's certain! The untrue foment dumbly
Disappears as soon as I imagine something
Abeyant to say: "I am a stranger to the
Effect of the City." For release from complex
Completion of opinion, I gulp the friendly
Beer. Starchy and too warm. "When you gotta travel
But are afraid to try, ignorance keeps you dead";
Not deliberate or wary, not rivalous,
He scales me again. Truth, which distends from his calm
Features, can preach that spleen was more obvious in
My confidence than in lineaments of his
Attitude. "And the City was never my home."
A relaxed mouth, he chuckles, "I wouldn't have known."
"Arkansas." "I'm from South Carolina myself.

Naw, not really. Just born there. We moved here after
That.” Contrasts define similarities the way
Strong silence defines important conversations.
I continue the private language of common
Agreement, “You recognize those sitting in the
Booth together?” “Yeh, they come here every night like
Me. They’re always griping. Giving shit to the drunks,
Too. And then if it ain’t about hippies, it’s blacks,
And if it ain’t that either, it’s politicians
Or bankers, or drinks got too Goddamn much water
In ’em, or this place stinks to high heaven. I don’t
Like hippies, and politicians ain’t worth nothin’,
But you don’t have to keep jawing about it. Did
You hear that shit about everything falling down
When they’re gone? I work ’cross the street from ’em, and the
Bunch sits around, shoots it everyday and yells at
Striplings not taking up slack for ’em, then raises
Hell if kids don’t collect what’s meant or can’t complete
It. Ain’t no changing a leech from being a leech.”

Confusion describes the eloquent passages
Of unbelief, truncates a continuous thought. . .
The faster he’s inspired! And I lose the method
Of thinking! Nothing retards difference, now and
Then, from touching rage with short, quick ambitions. What
Concord satisfies the provocation to hurt?

“That’s not fair.” Though I don’t sound committed enough,
He doesn’t need me too. “You Goddamn right it’s not.
Sure kids are loafers, but they’d work if they knew the

Practice. It's only a matter of trusting." He
Performs the stroking of a moustache; the story
He tells scares elocution low as though, somehow,
Antagonists could hear. Since the involuntary
Incidence of violence is so very vague,
Will even pleasure throw skeptics as nothing from
The minds of special men in next laughs anyway?

I pay and nod the kind of solitary nod
To my friend that says I want to find him again.
·No. Darkness inhaled parts of the City as we
Exchanged identities; and my heels leave no sound,
Since dissonance will invariably absorb
Rhythm. Cruel cities: you meet strangers if you
Need to receive someone, who, in turn, shall regress
Oddly to multiplication magnifying
The particular. I stir with strangers I can't
Omit, the completions we would have if just the
Selection which decides us were more precise. A
Clattering of bars enframes vagaries when, as
If closing curtains, a young driver locking a
Warehouse spreads a fence and ties the front with giant
Chains to build safety for the night. Such a fear, and
If not fear, how much generalization a
Driver endures and still corresponds to people!
Not fragmented, not imagined, but excellent
Defense! The lock on the chain snaps shut! Gutters, in
Fact, replete with yesterday, half wrappers torn and
Wadded, newspapers, a letter from an Uncle
Nicos on drastic paper. Ripped bricks lie in the

Street undisturbed, and slivers of glass exhaust the
Pavement; the naked bottles thrown at the lifeless
Sidewalk have unrelenting lids screwed tightly, a
Few buoyant necks still persevere. Where gray stores need
Paint, names are scribbled on walls with words that don't mean
A thing; and to be considered for a moment,
Which is not much to demand, a boy had primely
Crafted a signature. Two drunks asleep in a
Store mouth; one's like death, not sleep! The prepared eyes are
Open, blood's caked a swollen aperture, scratches
Beginning to scab grow to a sample cheek and
Neck. Why guarded silence pleads for an announcement?
Hair posed in sudden clots of dirt and glass; and while
I can smell sour clothes, toes are out of his right
Shoe, and the left's a mismatch. Pants rest oversized,
Two pair to degrade the shivering; holes all the
Way to his leg, despotic holes the wind's mean with.
Somehow, if objectively prudish, I despise
Him for letting me see peculiarities.

An experience is never quite vague enough
To be powerless. When knuckles tap my fingers,
An escaped capitalist advertises, "You
Got a quarter for food?" A bum demands the best
Of the worst of us. How to deny charity
For histrionic misery, but he's begging!
"I haven't eaten for a day. Can't you help me?
I haven't got much from my luck lately. You spare
Alittle loose change?" Every step he's routinely
Outwearing me; muscatel is a stiff vapor

From every pore, and his eyes are dim with results.
But defeat always needs obvious sympathy!
Yes! and I hurry to forget, and I leave him
Measuring over the special uses of a
Quarter. Having then been primely bitten by drunk
Disintegration, I uncover wilder-haired
Students at a protective corner who snigger
Me by and who institute trust by suspicion.

Store traits, smirched windows, shall ruin by drunken bottles
Thrown at darkness. Bitter faces, helpless faces,
Together are helpless faces needing help so
Badly they're hard; faces enlarged by disorder,
Faces carved alike. Police sirens howl their next
Hunt a few blocks away. North again. Over the
Progress of the segregated alarm, like the
Quite natural appurtenance of any sick
Building, a stick of a boy, pale and thin as bones,
Aberrantly leans from a slow, second-story
Orifice. Simply shaking, taunt, sweating colder,
Straining, ageless with hair hiding his age; and, as
If sirens were the only meaning, he yells, "Yes,"
From a laugh, "a Revolution now. We won't wait.
Racists, you've had your day. Fascists, again rotten
Retardants petrifying our chances into
Nothing and terror. Do you hear me? You've controlled
The planet too long." The veins in his neck twist like
A rope on his throat. Hysterically, "Do you
Hear me?" Shallow stares are spread with bloodshot. Then a
Girl, arranged with precise independence, and though

Restrained by such comfortable divination,
Reaches for the dedicated arm and whispers,
"John, they'll arrest you. You know that, don't you? They will."
Drugged with classical madness and, also, deftly
To abandon crippling confines of form, he jerks
Piquedly from the indifferent window: as a
Vague idea tried and dismissed, he disappears.
The girl, expansive in the freezing air, slowly,
Mechanically closes the obedient
Window; and she dispassionately then subsides.

My nerves cry selfishly in the realness of stone!
My creed: no one safely infers innocence from
My disillusionment. Slipping a deflated
Gradient, I am too weakened to consider
An escape, not from young melodramatists, a
Nestled herd hiding in the folds of a sack of
A building. Lonely people tend to speak loudly
Without courage or drama. Where can they sleep so
Primarily if they can not even trust each
Other? A hypothetical place to only
Survive? The influence most mildly left after
Everybody's taken parts of you isn't much:
Enough to love a girl, a drink, a walk a day?

But the City recovers in lights, relaxes
Where running great streets meet in a chaos of too
Many directions. As if happy, a woman
Struts swinging a vivid purse; and men joke about
Jokes I can't hear and turn for sparkling bars. The streets,
Open and different, ask me to hope again.

Laughing gross names and laughing nicknames but laughing,
Children beat tennis balls between vans, trucks in the
Distracted streets; cussed, yelling, rebelling, children
Cuss in return, almost damned when freedom is glimpsed
And lights bloom green. Loud and sweating dirt, they fly the
Avenue, soon press dirt-frosted faces against
Mirrorless glass and mock interiors, and know
Everything that'll happen and scatter before
It does. Yet a druggist screams from his bravest spot,
"You don't live around here. And now can't come back. You
Steal my best books." Indirection invites escape
For runaways. No, the tallest leader chances
An insulting lick with an awkward stick for a
Delivery boy who fights a bike with awkward
Plans; but escapees flit as though all were guilty.

The City is kindly releasing its people
And the people's other world; crowds breed and dissolve
Frenetically into the victorious
Rivers of humanity. I ride yielded and
Reckless, gladly betting on ourselves against the
Organization, intimidating all laws,
Twisting through organic car lines. Traffic lights don't
Bother herds. It's racking and dangerous as hell:
I can not even imagine the persuaded
Instructions of my gaze. Real speed's only used in
A limited emergency, but the City
Is an emergency for people to complete.

When a policeman in coveted shoes will lisp
A formula in a hurry, I hope he has

The fun he swears he will. Nothing succeeds within
The windstorm! Throbbing circles of people are dumbed
To staring at crisis. Pending, the addled edge
Promoting a much better view rustles at all.
Firetrucks and sentinels will surreptitiously
Separate a vulnerable station. And moans
Seep the crowds. Rumors. And the truth follows: a bomb
That'll blow out every floor is buried deep in
The terminal. Amid the slow search, hot boys roam
The percussion. Promptly everyone's bitter, mad
At police, the milieu, themselves, me. . .swells. Revolts
Still erupting somewhere, the gossip now passes
Sympathetically: "Take police from ghettos,
And the risk ends." Animating the one urge for
Freedom by listening, from impromptu guilt for
The perpetual and dangerous excitement,
I wander absurdly through events, people. "If
The police are not now openly removed from
The riots, new destruction will soon be running."
During the time that a drama prevails over
My conscience until an augury is exact,
Fear of death is calmer than fear of the City.

A preacher of an absolutely white collar
Screeches from a pair of teetery stools to the
Gathered expectants at the most unused corner,
"God will have His truth. If this shall be penitence,
He's coming to find us by noise and our weakness
For tricks even now. I hear Him exclaimed in brave
Scripture. What have we done? Repent should we turn God

Into a kind of hatred. We shall die by the
Hate we have given He will give back to us in
His immaculate judgment." Lifting a staff that
Steadies a nameless flag while evangelical
Eyes bulge when he closes them, "May God and Caesar
Choose conclusive mercy and atoning judgment."

To shake like an old maid! though everyone else has
The nerve to bitch at someone. As soon as I'm rife?
I don't want part of me, the part that's enraged, to
Talk for the rest of me. Who can accept any
Commotion without feeling it or not worry
Because of a consensus, sweat with somebody
Talking or not get mad at spontaneity?
I agree with timely convenience if I'm
Touching arms, saying excuse me because I add
To the great number, checking myself to see if
I've just improved or fallen; for small disasters
Occupy so much space and speculation and
The stuff that holds my body together wizens
Once again, although during other disasters
I forget I was ever alive the same way!

It's immortal to walk through crowds and, murmuring
Death if a bomb disrupts, to test the various
Senses I feel; surviving isn't the answer
For anybody; and more, close thinking about
The extant exercise is hard enough without
Accusatory statuettes of my unique
Limitations. Finally ambition alone

Rouses all rumors, some that will and some that won't
Come true; even finding half-truths that stay true is
Exceptional, but ever inescapable.
An inordinate suppression of triumphant
Confusion supports private chaos: we resort
To ceaseless movement when our movement is reduced.

Muscles shift as verdicts shift. Severe scandals die
With the death of excitement. It's true: scandals grow
If there's nothing else to do or if there's so much
No one knows the place to begin telling the truth.
From the first retreat by the police, barricades
And an ambulance and elusive taxis sift
Us; a businessman smiles at a stranger and, with
The anonymous voice he uses for strangers,
Dramatizes, "Will tolerance keep getting stretched
Thinner and thinner? We're insane to try to beat
The City at all." The stranger smiles back like a
Stranger and broods at the executive's stubborn
Gait. A public silence. Once waiting for any
Procedure with everybody, I look at those
Formal intentions on every side; once conformed
To delay, then radical response, I ride the
Crowd into the stomach of the station. Mother
Said many times, "If you're in a hurry to leave
Town, find somebody who doesn't live there, and it
Surely won't take you very long then to get out."

No, the fastest will return home regretfully.
Through the glaring size of the waiting room, higher

Than I bother to suspect and so wide I turn
Both ways to understand the worship, obsession,
Ever weighing its overweight, rejoices at
Its own convergence; and quiet recollections,
Laughs, and solicitudes ricochet hollow depths.
Moments that also swallow and calm my mind do
Not subtract me from the City and the quickest
Commitment to leave, a need that should define by
Now the lowest technique of conclusion. I'll search
Again for strengths, accept and use them until they
Are gone. Why is panic the first expression of
Memory as though we expected reaction
And then emergence? Girls I'd known, so easy to
Listen, once left me alone with times we had, I'd
Talked of our past so much we were prematurely
Lost in comparisons; how obvious it is
To be superficial as you crave an answer,
Advocacy! You hold to subtle resemblance
Of completion until you dissolve a prophet's
Voice with a death-grip, but still you can not release
Augury until it has died in front of you!
Gradually bled of the urge, you get weaker
Until you lie there in silent darkness staring
At the aspect you fear. I know the aspect I
Fear: a city, cocky city, full of order
Going everywhere, fugitives commanding speed
To hurry for the drastic good of the country.

But already two lovers do meet in a smile
And do not mumble about an interruption;

He anticipated all day the luxuries
Of her opinion. I flip from book into book;
Innominate pages then obfuscate to no
Meaning, and telephone directories are wrecked
On plans. As though I were struck by insoluble
Ignorance, any conjecture impacts as a
Vision and happiness depends selectively
On instant novelty so that the process is
Noisily apparent: "Operator, please, in
The area." And a hunt made beautiful by
The find: "Dobbs Ferry, Sir. That's Dobbs Ferry." I will
Locate friends by the tilt of an accident and
Derive a logic that ends progressive recourse.
"Dobbs Ferry! Dobbs Ferry!" How to get there? To get
Anywhere? Brag! Inviolate stupidity
Remains passive, though you shake inside until you
Get an answer. Will they be home? Or the phone's ring
Registered? Will prospects include a theory
That collapses? Amid hours when slight hints must
Completely come true, doubt's too strong to be idly
Entertaining. It's more a matter of time and
Presence whether friends can meet a wish; albeit to
Specialize in the foreign size of the station
Qualifies me as an expert on the City,
But knowing anyone will lessen my knowledge.

Someone opaquely disturbs several finished
Cigarette butts; he barely has a nod in the
Transparency of the crowd. The ticket line's for
Impatient aches: there is no acme to dissuade

From routine; stalked by clumsy bags and instruments,
Commuters and long travelers, the rich and the
Penny-counters, four handsome students and a fat,
Unscrubbed woman, defended by miscellany,
Compete for rewards of efficiency. Mostly
They fidget and don't quite ask a question, but stares
Perform an outrage for an agent who slowly
Counts light change or long tickets or if questions could
Be glibly finished elsewhere. An interruption
Paternally designed first obliquely adjures
Movement; even so it takes a long time to learn
The method of acting alone, and standing in
Line is forever! A squatty, scar-nosed man talks
For the rest of impatience, "Can't you hurry up,
Up there?" But the line's quick, only superlative
Length delays comfort. As long as a bald-headed
Clerk in the ticket cage sweats terribly among
Sneaking cold drafts of winter, he bemoanfully
Misses the sympathetic appetite of my
Glance; so I slur, "Dobbs Ferry." And he does spout an
Unconscious "Gate 3." The collection contains an
Ambition not so much for perfect umbrage as
For perfection, whenever people each trying
To protract a linear direction obstruct
Each other's design. Businessmen hustling to beat
The rush are causing it; information on tours,
Cameras, watches, cars, stocks advertises a
Medicinal painlessness; and brighter-than-live
Colors magnify the place they want me to
Go; stocks printed and new tickered reports besides;

Newspaper and hot dog stands by gross! Grand Central
Station! If a precise executive seems to
Sulk at my inefficient vagueness, crowds taking
A cue from success could turn on a stranger in
A second as he says something they never heard.

Across the station, descriptions manipulate
The extravagance of my theories; averse
Features invade the careful synthesis of my
Restless and sentimental prejudice. Gate 3. . .
Comfortable rejoinders descend across the
Tracks in steam and a dim definition, but the
Physique of the train displays Homeric symbols
And attitudes. Broken bursts of hot vapor must
Expel one more favorite recall's persistent
Odor, which, more than any image, inflates a
Recollection; for visions outline memory,
But smells open a hidden experience. Steam
Boiled tenderly in my sight many times, as I
Waited for a hoist to the adventure of a
First step; and the wilderness of a new world was
Delightful, because I was four, maybe five, round
And awkward like a new assumption. I held for
Dearlife to Hattie, another famous, but still
Ubiquitous grandmother. That I was burly
For my airy years never bothered her intent,
Since she'd lift me as she would a light paper bag.
I entertained myself by supposing trips were
Infinite, but they were brief connections from one
Part of the family to another; and all

Vicissitudes were replete with cogent style as
Well as delicious characters. If trains aren't much
Use anymore, they were heroes to her life; when
She started dying off, they did too; and as a
Function of the same recurring affection, my
Heroes will cheerfully die whenever I do.

For the first time today, I concentrate solely
On minor aspects, terse comparisons from the
Funereal protection of empty coaches
On my magnetic way to a smoking car. Though
Fumes irritate my head and my throat's racked, habit
Produces numb pleasure, and I need luxury
To depress a suspended modern age. The seats
Bear scars: inexorable sitting, leather cracked,
Knife hacks; so my skin wrinkles against wrinkles creased
For years. As soon as the varying stride of a
Train relaxes the leaden consequences of
Hostile remorse, with deep, tepid inhalations,
I can admire prospects for the future, because
I am young. I do not want to forget, just note
The City I've never seen and melt alittle.
Two men, who sanction themselves by ritual clothes
And the connotative material they read,
Agree an especial bond's weak. A bank wants more
Lease accommodations. But quickness is exchanged
For friendly ease; the two barters expertly fold
Always serious newspapers and mark gunshots
On the train. Impatient holes in the glass match the
Magnitude of a broad thumb! "It's more dangerous

For each trip. A friend of Joe Rutledge got shot in
The neck a month ago, and so far, they don't have
Anybody? It's no secret. Faceless boys in
Indistinguishable windows are firing on
These trains at random. Combined with rebellion there
Today, the chances should keep us from a train
Ride home. We're exposed in the worst areas." A
Mated sympathizer, haughtily simple at
The side, brandishing unwieldy fists, swallows, winds
The newspaper tighter than it should yield, and thus
Inures part of a flayed anger: "It's a zoo. Meat's
Thrown anywhere around here, and I'll be Goddamn
If half the City doesn't leap on top of it."
Justification quivers on his mouth. "Hell, war
Was extinct, then symptoms and punishment followed
Us home. And on the street, my God, I used to walk
Pleasantly to lunch and uncover a few friends
On the way. Now I step out of the building right
Into the African Olympics. What does a
Sane man do? I try to get along, really, but
People tell me to hire so-and-so to then keep
Someone off their backs, and I finally conclude
He can't accommodate the job. So I employ
Someone who happens to walk off the street for a
Change of scenery, and he is worse. Then the state
Employment service delivers one of its tree
Climbers, and, I'll be Goddamn, we still make money."
Vengeance disguised as logic is as merciless
As arrant vengeance. We abandon the opaque,
Underground arteries for darkness so firm my

Stare and rapid eyes rebound undiffused off the
Sullied glass. The emerging, empty buildings and
Shadows of poles effortlessly notch the passive
Distance we reduce. And though it has neither its
Voice nor an opinion, we smell the land working.

Conclusively a garbage color settles on
The remains and construction; uncolored shirts hang
Like empty bodies from fire escapes; and a torn
Off shudder. Black and near-black boys pee in more street
Water and do provoke fireplugs to lave away
Presumptive grime. An impassive woman who was
Once guaranteed an uncommon arrival stands
At a kitchen. The blocks will not suspend reasoned
Symmetry. People! people! The exodus of
The blacks from the guilt-wearied South confronts the North
With the impotency of self-righteousness, a
City's ambitions are hidden in ghettos. Clear
Suppositions asserting that I descry more
Negroes here than among placid or quixotic
Habits and land of Arkansas, that much larger
Multitudes are retained slavish behind austere
Windows inspire a sort of paralysis of
Detachment. Hardship is a poor method against
Mechanized quality. Outside my great, fissured
Glass, smoke drifts by the slow train: not raging, slightly
Coiling like a corpulent pile of rags on fire,
A pall thinner than wood burning is clumsily
Trailed by a dense smoldering of blunt rubber mixed
Combatively with metal and gasoline. Do

Destruction and fire implement a requisite
Purpose so that anger is consumed by modern
Conflagrations of purge? The circulating cast
Of a kindled cloud distends behind the City;
Bland buildings erected old. "It's very cold out
There, isn't it?" A priest's haunting, elastic voice
Continues the bribe stern preachers often enact
With grit, as if they would include me among the
Elite of a secret. "But the riots're just
Beginning. Every ruined edifice will burn
Before the honest reflex is exhausted. Just
The uninitiated are valuable there."
While the City's drowning head transfixes the taste
Of my concentration, any philosophy
Would persuade indifferently and, of course, too
Indirectly. Yes, a hometown fecundated
Robbed streets and normally enlarged families who
Wear immaterial houses; neglect was not
So efficient: Negroes don't evaporate! If
Pain creates a collective, there's no relief for
Private pain. "Burn it down?" My mind crunches on the
Complete question, but a dark pleasure finally
Says with smiles, " 'Cause they do it together. 'Cause they
Can do something together." "But they're not killing
The assailants. They're killing their own. Whenever
Anybody censures someone because of race,
People of his own race are murdered in one way
Or another. Do you believe that?" Among a
Collar so old it fails, performing layers of
His commentaries retain a political

Insistance. All questions do imply dissent, whose
Words clearer than I'm trimming commit: "The machines
Of prejudice are injured. And we recognize
The physical tricks of history, formulas
Negroes confront, the effects of hope on human
Nature. Ghettos, the newest categories for
Justice?" Comfortably wrapped in concentration,
The priest prefers to singly conclude another
Definition, "There were those who cared, who cared so
Much that when they saw the first killing at night long
Before, the honesty of their presentation
Claimed them victims: sequestered, illegimate,
When conspiratorially everybody
Else was making it together, stealing, buying,
And preaching, calling everybody's confusion
Laziness. Yes, there were some who knew, but they were
Uncommon for a very common time. Joking
Antipathy for leadership, the promotion
Of mediocrity; why is peace powerless
When there is a general distrust of pity?
Good familiar hatred exhibits the mad
Comfort of passive opportunity, and peace
Reflects vacantly until it's easier to
Expect than the lethargy of hate. Is peace taught
Like propaganda? Injected like medicine?
Using the tools of power and deforming the
Messages? No, neither politics nor modern
Policy is an option for the Church. When the
Importance requires no debate, the Church's one

Reply must be unmistakable. However,
Jurisdiction appeals even to saints." Like a
Slap, he accosts me, hinting condemnation could
Instead inspire my voice, "What are you going to
Do?" Sanctimony intends a caricature,
But well before the severity is fully
Remedied by mercurial comedy, he
Evades his own askew game, "This is my stop. Not
Far from the freeless exorcise of tyranny.
But here we breathe the results, swollen air and more
Conspicuous refuge. I don't believe distance
Can be permanent. Stay well. Still think of the rare
Question, what if nothing taught peace. See, the outcome
Of today's discord is so meticulously
Unimportant. The preservation of the great
Alternative is found irresistible." Since
Humans will apply time to defy defects of
Conviction, he gladly snaps a flippant "good-by."

The tracks trains ride lie down bare, gray like small, fallen,
Winter oak trees. Among more grass and rocks, poses
Change less. Smoke doesn't curl, but floats ominously,
Following the river to richer towns. And while
We pretend a mad, blindless sniper merely mocks
And will excuse the best of us, he'll greet a train
Dealing torment to his city in garbage-soaked
Ghettos sleep can ruin more, because sleep makes him
Dream. Once thoughts can rave, I imagine seditious
Clarity behind glassless windows! And scatheless,
With penetration anesthetized, voyagers

Read on, reflect on justifiable blindness,
When fires are burning nearby, mysteriously
Burning resentment. Dull coldness and dense rage pass
Dangerously through my style. Shutting my eyes to
Calm them down, I suspend editorials; but
Amid a lair, Old sayings pop, and old sayings
Pop rhetorically, "And all those people with
No value in their dignity have no meaning
In their pity. . .all those people with no value
In their dignity will have no meaning in their
Pity." It fits: we harbor hushed declarations
That advocate our extremely private pleasures.

Although they prefer freedom to habit, riders
Surrender neatly to implied intellection.
What beast, if a beast, would crave those who once slip in
Death-sleepy eyes to instant cars, waiting empty,
Authorized? Even illumination contains
Approval by darkness, no further than sealed tree
Lines impounding the mouth of night! So much careful
Indirection directs lures to dispel weather's
State legends: courage drawn from bright spots in the dawn;
How noon turns itself over slightly warmer; and
Western tincts raise alot of sundown. Power is
A fact facts can not reflect, for the claims of all
Detail are the remainder of former desires.

Fireplaces glow on the tracks. Dobbs Ferry. A town's
Name is a story too; trips across a river
Two hundred years ago rise to a crystal-steel

Freeway leading people by restive progress now:
Modernity heaves taller than mud, stronger than
Rickets enervating siderails of the floating
Bridge, and anybody can get anywhere from
The luxury of conveniences. The last
Ferry captain's dead; no one remembers his red
Hat donned for authority, his progenitors
Buried and breathing here; a daughter's a waitress,
A grandson's a druggist of Omaha, drilling
For gas, plywooding in Oregon? By chance, if
Origins forecast descriptions of death, the town
Suffers too much from an overweening mother.
Shaping the past for a better future, building
The young to excuse and commit to the old, the
Town politicians composed a fable, and each
Generation mimes an inorganic version.
At the inversion of estimated prowess
Into gluttonous separation from lucid
Society, the replicas of exclusive
Sentiments enjoy provincial stature. For blocks,
Houses do not slowly falter obtrusively
From equivalent complexions, where all nightly
Evidence of near-criminal nature is then
Cited on notable porches, and muted lamps
Balanced in a window's performance are further
Dulled by linen curtains; somewhere within manners
Of a family crime inside the prostrate rights
Of anonymous gates, a ritual will have
Ordered the players to continue presumption
And marry their own and have their own kind. I've seen

It: gathering at a threat when closing is first
Complete, they will never ask anything again
For which they do not already know the answer.
Born to evasion, they preserve servility. . .
But that's not enough! An obvious submission
Isn't tolerable! Protecting each other
For themselves? Most members collectively deny
Commonality, but a few witness too late
They're servants to idolatry they organize.
If corrected by insatiable systems,
They discard reforms; the radical process yet
Absorbs them restfully. They're the institution
(Labor hoards value), and they die each time they stop
Working. And as compensation, immunity
Was all they expected, and it nullified them.

While I wander without close plans, search revokes search
Imitating stone. Though hushed by a compromise
With the environment, an air of conflict rests
In premonition; should hate select a burning
Form, suffering would cry a special way here? The
Answer's simple though rhetoric: leave craftsmen to
Technique; for they, self-applauding, volunteer quaint
Ambiquity at fast, outrageous prospects.

Near another graceless crossing and attending
A rhapsodic hitching post, by an iron gate
He might enter for a home, the old man freely
Luxuriates in familiar streets and true
Directions and shudders on an impartial cane;

Advice insinuates rich safety, if pronounced
By old men, who as experts of oldness only
May claim obeisance for patriarchal remarks.
Lest relaxed clothes hardly grip an inattentive
Body, a patched workshirt and irascible pants
Under a limp-long coat splice at a flamboyant
Waist-rope; not like coxcombs, he'd invoked happiness
To an old-age process. "Heber?" he asks himself.
"53 Heber? The Anthony manor? Yes,
After heathens raised apartments, the lessons of
The family vanished, and again precedents
Were corrupted by a surge for profit. The house
Is now empty of history, because fads mete
Bad charm. The strangers are parasites, who invade
Tender places and donate the bright remains of
Luxurious habits. The home's now dull, though new
Objects dominate the grass." "I want to find my
Friends." "There's too much expectation. People will stray
There like, well, I never can recognize the same
Process and I pass twice a day. Over the hill,
Down three blocks, then a right, first house on the right." The
Last sentence blasts as literal memory from
Affection for knowledge: of paint change, scandals and
Witty fiction, decay and healthy promises
By candidates, of timid, unalterable
Patterns, imperious jealousy — all constant
Reminders dissension will often expose an
Object of prejudice as an example of
Oppression. And tottering to consecration
And unconscious anecdotes on the part of a

Once more homogeneous town, he, like a friend,
Had calmed my disordered urge. Not by convictions
He applied but by events he selected, I
Anticipate this didactic series: the old
Man was old men I had known, and the compulsion
That prompts me breathes slower; he became my justice.

Changes? Mary-Helen will again fall quiet
For Victor's words to avoid suspicion, since there's
No temper, no concession, an indefinite
Affair; changes he'll analyze until they're flat.
How we test by tender guile; when ideas read
Sympathies well, faith can resort to arrogance.

I retrace of Victor's fakery a comic
Incongruity: "Sex is free and physical.
If any stranger kindles you best, why repress
The body's stimulus? Mary-Helen and I
Understand about unproven morality.
And she knows I've gotta try if I encounter
A woman to travel." The modulating voice
Transparently toppled weaker and deeper, "For
Her, the same freedom prevails." As I remember
The nondigressive cycle of events, there was
A genteel woman available among soft
Opportunities at an exaggerated
Party; and because experts need exhibition,
Victor followed her involuntary charm. Now
I, richer for variation, weighed the exchange
Of adultery for prudery, though surely

Fiction, curiosity, liquor, prize, each an
Honorable talker, extenuated me
To Mary-Helen, entertainment to quickly
Entertain. Oblique notes of jealous outrage were
Sounded! From such a warm doctrine as rational
Revolution, the liberal philosopher
Will also be the conservative lover. So,
Escaping pressures of theory, Victor, in
Fact, who, reverting to home notions, collected
Mary-Helen like another gray coat, withdrew
From gamesmanship. Early next morning, pliantly
Separating my attention from solid sleep
Began a silent, subtle apology: first
Requital for the progressive couple who, as
Ascetic repentants from deserted statements,
Produced a liberal breakfast for appeasement.
From denouement easily derived, truth also
Appears carefully simple — the way patterns and
Inevitability of conflict succeed
Compromise. A whip of a mouth, he is almost
Standard to major themes of these times: "The only
Revolution is from my freedom to yours." Just
As freedom illustrates particularity,
Maybe he's right in the long try: "To convert and
Free someone automatically alters an
Institution." Not quickly convertible, a
Speculator in the name of Freud, favoring
Self-justification to our tolerance, he
Isolated compassion from us. Now most do
Consider hylic religions; yet he, less sure

Than the favorite analysis he propounds,
Though still stronger than approvers who let success
Teach them, nimbly will solicit abstract power,
Gratuitous freedom, generalized logic:
"New York's the brave city. Fresh to anger over
Cliches, it nourishes on invention and the
Promise for honesty. Since fear's not applied as
An excuse, events can meet maximal desires,
And each act of transference is reprimanded.
I will exhibit any remark I ever
Value." The dialectics of optimistic
Experiment are by now resolved. Paint peeled to
Dirty boards does lament with a warped balcony;
A long-awaited choice degrades in importance
Before those artifacts evincing time's relief.
The urge to sleep and talk bites again, whenever
I imagine fruitful faces that slowly nod
Renewal and invite a ceremony of
Recollection. Should Victor and Mary-Helen
Rove? Through the night? No! Around the house, a snooper,
Feeling as a burglar feels out prospects, perplexed
By the taut energy of alternatives, I
Eventually stand before a door that's a
Monument. Neither exploding nor preening on
The ferreted absolution, I will slowly
Complete the trip and tap: quit, louder, quit, Louder.
"Nobody there, fellow." A voice like hell contains
Me; tilted over the nervous parapet, an
Overripe woman severely hangs there braless
Under a dress that fits like a thin tent. Her hair's

An unkempt hedge; scaled knuckles on the freezing rail.
"They ain't in." I'm yelling, "Where are they?" "I wish I
Knew. In the middle of the night it must have been,
They packed and deserted us." Decisions crisply
Unravel once the present stops being the last
Promise; previously braced by conjecture, I
Now stabilize the remaining propositions.
She adds instrument to injury, "Yes, I called
Her daddy. He is a surgeon somewhere in the
City. He doesn't know either, and he won't pay
The bill. They're gone. Plain gone." What do you do if the
Last wish fails? Absolutely nothing; yet because
We prefer reality to intention, I
Collect my inheritance and enlarge prideful
Movements. As the last of hope declines, inference
Tends to miss; it takes a strong belief for us to
Think clearly. Mute to contemporaneity,
The deadness goes about confiscating desire,
Energy, method. Children play with fun amid
My concentration. What inquiring laughs briefly
Tormenting do resound! And hence I countervail
A city that's not just craven and brutish as
A maniac on my mind but will shoot me down
Like an unleashed dog if I'm at the wrong place at
The wrong time; I've already learned it'll quell me
When I disagree with a facile attitude,
But it'll buy me a drink or a plate of food
If I don't: so, for the sake of procession or
Silent survival, you better be a pretty
Damn good lier if you still plan to break even.

Ideology and money aren't expected
To reach love; but results seek more love should someone
Be a bored demagogue and use all precious things,
Because someone else prizes them. Victor, who snatched
People by their suspicions, could avoid any
Final encounter; with our worn fringes ever
Relatively loose, we aren't absolute, but he
Obsessed one idea to beat the confusion;
To fail with Freud implied misery, even though
Philosophy can only verify, can not
Initiate. "To be complete," he said. But now
Exposed, he returns to ambiguity; and
Despite nods from self-control, anybody who
Thinks always being right will save him is lying.

At least bad weather doesn't step heavily; oh,
I shook occasionally with winds, and when I
Blew into my hands, fingertips cracked into peaks.
But a pluck of a man invites me to the cold
Rivet by slapping himself to beat the sting out
Of a cloth coat. All digits contract for stiff fists
Inside moth-eaten gloves. Punctuated by a
Pair of dripping earflaps, a crumbly cap string-ties
Under a florid face, which had harvested pits
Like pockholes. Over the vulnerable flesh, a
Yellowy crust lies: long years in the cold produced
Formal resistance. Though a throat earns him dimes, he's
Paid for coarse and mean noise that will try now. One day
Follows the same day, each year shall mimic the next
Reaction, and animation fondly marks the

Perfunctory recall, he never missed working
One. Ennobling the loath mien, a new scarf should flare
Heroically but infrequently; lost by
Oblivion, a well stretched cap at home smiles like
A badge; still stamina grows keen, because one thought
Extends further than worn obstacles. Leaning on
Cold's wonted pain to fight the cold, coughing a sale,
He snaps a newspaper double on his wooden
Chest and judges, "Thank you, young man." "Riots Will Prove
Worse Without Rain," headlines remark, surmising that
Milieu more than untrue superiority
Contributes to disorder. Just as Darkness begs
For light, just as bones steadily beg for sleep or
Food, confusion, evoking wild political
Power from paralysis, begs for clarity
To give meaning to confusion; no one is sure
Pandemonium is good instruction, albeit
Bigots do infer suffering teaches me my
Appointed place. A mouth's open; I do not hear
The report. Tracking aimed rails, I lift myself to
Platforms for a return, which is not a return
At all but recompense for not confirming a
Friend; neither intolerance nor an invention
Relieves arbitrary law. Sweet boxes for more
Greenhouses? Luxurious cattle cars steer the
Conscience home. Before families can wilt under
Darkness of a real night, they will cozy toward
Honey-fed babies and assign uniqueness to
Blunt children. Contrasted against whining trains jammed
To unanimity, a few loners wait for

The next instinctive, city-minded train; I don't
Know the loners, but that's not important, I'm one
Of them: night performers and night watchmen; women
Who will primely entertain by soliciting
Entertainment; a custodian who follows
Accidents, extravagant in the City. All
Wailing great sounds of the train shall inspirit the
Suicidal attraction of power; as if
Bravely freed from the mute celebration of night's
Inertia, through giant sways shaking flakes free from
Routine wood, an empty train tears other echoes
Out of our passive ears. New weight is cradled through
Intuited doors; imbued at a special neck
Blain, a pregnant woman, gladly careful for her
Imperiled conception, enjoys that life alone
Can imagine life. Assaulted motorcycles,
Rippling on mythological plats and barking
Fumed earth inside the darkness, are weapons in the
Hands of the assaulted. In just the manner of
Molding philosophy to fit fastidious
Pleasure, I consume specific elements for
Fastidious moods. Against a contemplative
Language, an aggressive train gulps the opposite
Track, but another lone locomotive agrees
With our direction; if options are the symptoms
Of liberty, then regulations will emerge
As shibboleths for captivity. During a
Newspaper preaching that reality always
Overwhelms good sense, extremes further attract my
Self-saving: arrests of childish victims and the

Immunity of criminals; looters stuff their
Pockets by toys and liquor; from the apex of
A gun, madly discharging history's curse at
History's neutrality, miscellaneous
Snipers mislay several didactic bullets;
And from the dead, encircled by prodigal blood,
Aggrieved innocence further grieves. Death that stops an
Argument also keeps customary order
Operating. Political power is marked
To mute inarticulate articulation:
Police horses trampling closest to the loudest
Simply teach the unpatriotic lesson that
Governments will counsel by threat as well as by
Colloquy. A dramatic commissioner says,
"Smoke will die if hazardous winds do not increase."

Inside this half-asleep head, my dull eyes invite
The night. Defining darkness with so much random
Incandescence, like scattered stars over naive
Fields, a tiger's across the land, and two rabbits
Peer at each other; I see a solitary
Giant wing without a bird to dignify; a
Laggard of strong crossed-knees, of a vile fedora
Hiding vile thoughts, delights in the convenience
Of the image. If viewed for various angles,
The passing of lights, evanescence, fulfills the
Irony of the organizationally
Powered cities. How long for more generalized
Discovery, institutional lessons, or
A controlled gadding will repetition always

Resort to velocity, while introduction
Pends so indomitably deliberate? Such
A plump and wrinkled pair, still heart-bitten, chuckle
For secret's sake and forbid each other passage
To more audible tokens, hidden by their mock
Discretion for suppressed revelry. Lovers will
Be duped by love's praxis: statements are easier
To identify when they're disguised. Tittering
Whispers, made of love's-exacted twins, establish
Jack, whose craft they inaptly displayed: "He'll catch hell,
But he deserves it, the blustering clown. Only
Conceit can stand him when he's candid. Let him bitch
Some more. Can't you hear him, Harry? Clamor will fit
Him like comfortable clothes: 'Your work is my work.
And if you don't refine it, I will ride your back
Until you win.' " All love divides into fractions:
Incomplete circles, abrupt forms, everything love
Hasn't been keep lovers whole. The other half, then,
Staring a defective laugh, closes the story,
"I'll bet one of the owners explored the blunder
First. You recognize Jack's whipped-dog look 'cause he did
Not know the reason for all the bellow?" For what
Moiety of famine lingers deadly after
Separate diffusions merge, and, once again, such
Emptiness was righteous for filling? Awkwardly
Event-twins assure with contiguity once
More: breath-shared exile, one more exchange of absolved
Details reduce anarchy of quaintly selfish
Dimensions. But I must settle for happiness
I steal; and yet a deserted train screeching on

Behalf of a deserted city isn't much
Of a bargain. I'll question accidents for no
Universal moral: I couldn't willfully
Stand the commonplace. We're damned if necessity
Discounts the generic or if ever, near death,
We gamely tell the sad truth for peculiarly
Minor reasons. Headlines divine, "Riots Will Get
Worse"; where, night on night, solitude anticipates
Violence from tyranny of hints, no patent
Conclusion can bisect violence and desire.

Sleep confounds me if I worry about sleep; though
Safety is not as dangerous as ignorance,
It's twice as fragile if we preserve protection
As a rule. So there's neither destination nor
Sanctuary amid desperation and the
Trance. Disorder fully elicits physical
Priorities of a generation: freedom
Projects the size of lust, and for authority,
Quick eclipse no matter how facile. Gray haze but
Hanging on skeletal tracks recites the lesson
For hurried pleasure: with no reason, all moments
Can turn cruel. Too, as yet even ungracefully,
Original motives are ever modified,
Contorted or rarefied. A city disparts
Into dependent apostates who speculate
To ransom control; but, at last, all suspicious
Regard will, of course, check the ruler, not the ruled.

No rush. No torn people. Nothing to verify
Margins of danger and mood here. Advocating

Individuality of habits also,
The conductor, bolting, bumping, coughing, scolding,
Illustrates the athletics of primacy. Where
Shrilling to jerking stops, a train shortens the range
Of personal power; clumsily, two soldiers
Scramble at the dreamless door, which opens with a
Call to remember more than sin; for we love to
First be dutiful to quirks. Giant ramps echo,
My deaf heels click like metal, and in far corners,
Clouded caverns blithely confess to the absence
Of obscurity: two teenage boys with hair wild
As grass attempt terrible masks to be wild and
Melt into silence. Escape leaves voids; thus, loose sounds
Gather, clattering over dissonant tiles and
Settling at the mosaic pools of my feet. More
Softly than desertion, uncertainty gnaws in
A long hall: I recognize sample rhythms of
My breathing; I cough a speck, scratch and apprehend
My fingers rake my palm; when I shuffle, clunking
And swishing encourage bold revelations to
Arrest all misery in the newest game of
Happiness; uniquely I jump, and several
Repressed children I disguise applaud; unfinished
Sneeze, muffled yawn, disjunct trills, characteristic
Of parts in search of colligation, carom on
Single echoes until one twitter dominates;
To blat unconsciously, the history of a
Blare would overbear earth's every sounded report.

Successively mingled among the praedial
Pragmatism that gains more by neglect than by

Enterprise, as strayers prowl a predatory
Daze, which better invites an humble curio
Who always yields and withdraws where executives
Savor secrets' ritual and fraternity,
And while they whose ambition pleads for modesty,
Whose meek punctuality elevates honest
Success, acknowledge trains going anywhere go
Nowhere in particular again, an endless
Reminder forbodes Fate: to those who prepare for
Suffering, suffering is done without remorse.

Lights disguise time and lie about primitive sleep;
Great lights, surrounded by tubercular darkness,
Can still convince you it's day. But I know, lack of
Sleep has no challenge left. Quite naturally and
Unawares, salvation procreates the nearest
Exit to night, less known than empty, dogmatic
Spaces. Ponderous plans making obscurity
Home; finales of doors, bistros, convenience;
Conspicuous talents; all are bid trite good-bys.

Night strengths blurt first my bald zest and then my fresh birth.
Taxis, happy and dull screams, crass machinery
Establish apparent circumscriptions of state
Subways and buses that still daunt angular calls.
Night sounds for disenamored ease? They're part of day!
Subtle flickers and huddled bodies cramp a wall:
Seven hustlers, old men and women who adopt
Practices of old men rub fretted hands over
Burning newspapers and cast cards into quick piles.

Lest warmth oppress completely by staid default, one
Of two scamps who feast on gloves shares wealth with the numb.
Those who don't play have a favorite anyway;
Yet those who bet pennies and nickels praise self-styles.
One practiced grab captures the elusive pelf of
A warm dollar with kings over nines. Five-card draw.
Briefly shrinking lower for the fire's last remnants,
They cuss someone more for failing than for quitting.
Should gambling gratify seductive vagrancy,
The concept of reality can not endure;
Don't they know that if they could win each fast wager,
The small proportion of the game dilates panic,
Where all jade or erupt at minor flippancy?
Crisp with desuetude, dun papers no longer soothe.

Drawing a road from where I stand, permanent change
Applies multiplicity as prime instruction.
Objects and I blink at each other gawkily;
Cans and sign poles momentarily mean fashion:
They're other places, hyperbolic by distance,
Remembered approximations of lawless love,
Antecedent streets more matchless than correct that
Claim happiness is not is, but was or will be.
Variety also includes indecision
And impotency, can abet imperatives
By obfuscation; yet no perplexed longing tests
Later workers selling experience as Self.
One woman bothers to devise an ageless pose;
Mien denotes she either slaps up or mops up food.
Worn is pluralism that's been yelled at plenty,

But Roundness incarnates fair thoughts that note too much;
Enunciation flows through her short, thick body
That, perched wart-like, rules from an abrupt appendage;
With cropped hair, clumsy working clothes, a crumpled snack,
She proposes an easy talk and easy joy,
Not because we're alone and therefore directed
To talk, nor because I know her or know she knows
Me, but because we recognize that each of us
Holds the best we are for the most private moments;
Nothing reforms idealizers of silence;
For they know everything can happen, and they know
Simple ways and hard ones, how to cheat to stay safe,
How if you're weak pride'll get to you, how to cheat
And be honest. By these subtle smiles from afar,
Politically wistful stares won't quite persuade:
She would keep asking for modified dissonance;
Only those who've believed neither faith nor magic
You always scare with eyes, philosophy, manner.
"By 3rd Avenue gets me closer to the car."
When she awoke to my fundamentals steely,
I reduced all prospects to a declaration.
"Walk this street to the church. I'm waiting on a bus
To Queens. If early, I watch police patrol like
They live here where nothing happens. How far on 3rd?"
"Far." Thus plagued by a foreign code of measurement,
I rather identify naiveté a spot.
"It's a flimflam and paralyzed city, you know."
Though better inspiration will deny trouble,
Old women can placate no young man's paradox.

Resurrected dying without sleep, I accept
Incongruities if they are exceptional
And kin to natural laws or orgasmic faith.
Remains of a very rude beer tears my stomach.
Somehow negation welcomes derision as a
Rule that performs justly for the social task of
Adjusting to Revolution or bigotry.
I've absorbed corners where lights plead liberation;
A concise woman, who apparently forfeits
The formal luxury of provinces women
Save like bankers or children with an only toy,
Is encouraged by a mock-scotty, which is not
Even a dog but an urge she's miniatured.
Precious things seek a well organized parish, yet
Among novelty's suasion and assault of the
Merciless equality of a wilderness,
Regularity is first signs of a death wish.
When cities treat politics with an actor's flare,
No wonder then dogs deign to deem us as equals?

From a period of lights, restaurants and bars
Reduce crude desires to crude possibilities;
Counting boys as bashful customers, girls shine too;
No families or children to still the caprice,
A young sloucher being casually single.
Of homes too empty to be dwellings, jokingly
Equating manner with felicity, language
With secrets, Puerto Ricans inherit the streets;
Sons have learned to lean like fathers who learned to laugh
At laughing. Down into the night I quickly touch,

Skies, more remote, posit the incomplete answer
To faithless prayers, which will resort to degrees of
Lust committing us first to survival and then
To failed vague principles of success. Stars blinking
In shadows retard the gross articulation
Of bricks and recover the part of freedom that's
Almost a quiet winter night in the fields where
A starved, country wind is a dog howling for space.

Street lamps isolate darkness; slowly mere presence
Will void chaos by reflecting the kinetic
Ambition of material. Willful subjects
Intimidate and beguile a thinker, who, for
No other wish, I guess, than to be eccentric,
Will consider Essence always beyond his own
Physical dimensions? Hence not as old as he
Wants to be, a bent, unbendable man uses
A post more as a place to be than as a prop.
A beer can sloshing gathers fingers of a hand
The way inebriant attracts hypothesis;
He scratches with the fleshy ferocity of
Delinquents; if not brave or verbally thriftless,
He's less vicious than cynics who pretend to be
Brave, less meticulous to secret pain than I,
Who flick away systematic priorities
Of night by lecturing myself on strict rewards
Of suffering. He shares a tin cough; even sealed
Sounds can not keep from defining the litany
Of symbols: bits of frozen mud under a shoe
Are snapping like twigs — cause looks unsafe or it's spurned.

People disappear, not because the night's older,
But obscurity has drifted too far where I
Snatch occasional light off evading taxis
Or such illuminated guardians that scare
Away clumsy thieves. A surge of youth relieves fixed
Qualities, but can't be quite so sincere; for like,
Young ages ply incestuous dependency
As a participant means to descry themselves:
Turning submissive minds on weakness is worse than
Obscurity. All the night has propounded but
Individual requests, as though we were tried
Not for our lives but for more punctilious sins.
Cautiously included in bowels of the City,
Even acute observations are abnormal.
Preliminary sounds hide in bare-shred whispers
Of the corner, up an alley, behind a wall?
Resonant, hollow, atomic, vicinal, deft
Orders are impelled by insinuation, since
Law is easily taught; but I can't save a bum
Who lies coatless in thin sheets of ice on rare weeds.
To help means the choice to publicly violate
Fears of denial; but silence, like the bum who
Is stuffed with self-important pity and crying
For more, whose moans tap my bones, learns that, among moods,
Ingratiated capitulation is greed.

Like rat eyes, like cats of normal condescension,
Dead eyes break from monotony and squint stunned that
I bother to contradict a night with the cold
Worse than divination! Stiff chinks select proud noise. . .

Night accents pale things: half-lies that demonstrate the
Truth only when we expect to hide them again;
Intuitions that never quite make it to an
Idea; escalated wish as laziness.
Where old darkness solves the pure violence of our
Incongruity by slowly revealing pure
Uncertainty and fear from our parochial
Sanity, undefinable authority
Rejoices at generality, because if
Truths are the same length, old brokers continue to
Match choices with false history. I passed here as
Misshapement could get worse. Now a dog commonly
Starved hunches at fence bars and sniffs for a bitch; no,
A scavenger fully suspecting purity
Is most desired by destruction fantasizes
That blown warmth and next correction are drawn in waste.
Distant cars muffled by the City resemble
Forms too close; adventures of overgrown, childhood
Games realized in conceit. Manacled stores, bars
With no alcoholic signatures but rather
Evidence of stoic self-preservation can
Estimate the sovereignity of the various
Hours and attitudes of a day. Learning from
Architecture the techniques of those physical
Defenses against unpleasant winds, bums rely
On the ingenuity of curves and angles.
Austerely rhythmic, lucky drunks are very drunk
Or drinking. A human effect talks only with
An arm and begs for penury samples of my
Superiority; I crisply regard guilt

As an invasion of solitude; so, featly
Avoiding mute claims on my peculiar faith,
I particularize general affections
Of human nature to placidly mean my own
Protection; still I know ambiguity is
The first result of mercy. Thus, all objects shall
Indicate rescue and constraint, and I gaze at
The red deterrence of a sign; visions from past
Objects act like glances from forbidden power.
Radical contrasts provide a cold stone head, if
You knowingly submit to a perpetual
Argument or, from a hard concentration on
Aptitude, anticipate reductions of the
Body's aptitude; formal as wood, as quickly
Anesthetized as darkness, with everything and
Absolutely nothing telling me to fear the
Details, I can not modulate extremism
In the physical particular! Hot smooth blood
Riots my eye and tears me dizzy busted blank
Against the broken and deserted symmetry
Of a hall; waiting hushed to be tempted, a sear,
Lean razor rests on the right side of my throat; the
Crack in the wall swells my back. Just like rats out of
A coign: "Boy, what you got?" A mouth steams with sweat and
Hair shielding such bleach and intemperate skin; how,
Naturally, desperation, the gentle cause,
Is nevertheless restively illustrated
In oppression. From what defeat is it best to
Implore? Candor eliminates the last vested
Defense that's subtlety: "What do you have we want?"

The other thief, white-flushed in shadows, has pressed hands
Over my contour, squeezed and hurt; he first grumbles
Working with a short smile as though he enjoyed me.
With infectious pain now ascending orderly
In a twisted arm, I mention I ache from the
Skill of deliberate violence; but hackneyed
Administration of control celebrates the
Masterful inhibitions of egotism:
"Where'd you get that accent? The City doesn't much
Recognize a mysterious manner like yours.
The weather will get haughty tonight. So you line
Over to a two-dollar hotel. We'll select
What we need and leave the rest, but the prizes go
To our good cause: we live off society's greed."

Engines of blood pound through the avenues and old
Systems of reconciliation. The greater
The evidence the lesser the chance there is for
Compromise and elemental union; for I
Jabber completely until I can't wish and the
Rest of my glands of modification surely
Collapses. Awful tears uncontrollably grow
And design the facile allusions of my glare.
I try to release the experience; there is
No one to hear the elucidation of the
Riddle that includes a common desire for the
Natural law to characterize an event
As an organic truth. From dimness, thieves, mumbling
Of Madeline sleeping while I lie here paceless,
Forget what questions they leave so long unanswered

By guarding safeless motives. Shame accompanies
Celibate sobs, dying off among regardless
Time I need: time to simplify myself, time to
Get away without being caught again by the
Provincialism, a long time for milieu to
Establish arrogance for rescue, which would thus
Accumulate a mock stranger casually
To intrude and comfortably relieve darkness —
Someone I can't detain, but can trust his noisy
Deflections to loosen the ascetic silence.
Rising, I collect my keys and wallet and wipe
Tears dried to my mouth, as though I estimated
Degrees of my innocence by tell-tale spots of
Grief; yet remarkably energetic, even
Attentive to ways small features fit together
To produce secondary movement, I choke on
The remains of accidental catharsis and
Redemptively accept, categorize the street.

An invited visitor already departs;
Clean, swift clicks to a heel distantly cut around
A loud corner and intimate the temptation
Of community in a desert. My senses
Slowly redefine like eyes that awaken to
See a paradox and the same figures in much
Clearer light, that interpret captions of even
An absurd night: catcalls, scratches and raking that
Make passive fright. Though reasons can aptly display
The loci of many faults, they can not alter
The indomitable Status Quo by strictly

Instructing subjects to declare themselves bad: the
Immoral are, generally speaking, the first
To recognize their immorality; resting
Bricks and serrated walls, neutralized by age, will
Consciously stand and defy the dominion of
The precise mind that assumes only clarity
Can determine future directions of every
Indeterminate victim. Proximity blends
Again with each thought: the night's gray, the closed moon must
Now be brimming, salvation is quietly caught
In the identity of lemon peels and the
Beer cans, which clog the curb. As remaining night life
Hustles to each one's darkness and a rat or two
Gnawing hurry in a corner and two human
Eyes, glassy-blank with interest and defeat, lie
Close to the rats' craft of escape, insanity
Does appear possible in every episode
Of circumstantial unreality. Yet it is
The habitual evidence of our costly
Mortality that verifies the illative
Qualities of our endurance. With a longish
Muscle declaring its unique condition, my
Arm throbs irregularly again; and further
Accompanying my boisterous wing, as a stern
Window raps fluidly shut spitting rotten wood,
Which scatters eagerly, love and lovers now have
A second and inferior look in a shocked,
Submissive apartment. What is the subtle and
Convincing dispute between approximations
And memory if, for both, I appropriate

Results well before I am posed with the question,
Or if vistas impersonate familiar
Neurosis, or if interpretations repress
Bits of information so that emotions won't
Spin off in every direction from my arrant
Inebriation and leave me paralyzed? Shall
I encounter the embodiment of my dark,
Deep neglect? Is fear a wish consummated or
Ineffable crimes concluded for normalcy?

Under seeping smoke, phantasms effortlessly
Puff on next-to-last cigarettes in an obscure
Corner of an alley, a bend in a building,
Or from the pile of bricks; the great cloud, like a shrewd,
Suspended spirit, by thinning higher giving
The night a shade of gray, blends uphill with manic
Tenebrity until I can't match the careless
Difference between darkness and low, white-drifting
Smog. Everything's contained by ashen and famous,
Ethereal obscurity, which denies trust.

Parking bulbs flashing! The osmotic tenderness
Of Little Car I glorify as an unfed
Calf pitifully choiceless would yield to instinct
And leave the judging to free things. Estimating
The crescendo of recognition, I fumble
And deride my elusive keys; foretasting as
Though the car were a girl I haven't seen for a
Long time, I project memoirs of delicious yet
Finite history into the dimensionless

And unscientific future; if collective
Systems try to stop unpopular opinions,
The car's a way to be lost, until traveling
And evanescence become a brutal cult of
Popularity themselves: lonely journeys then
Enact anarchic conceit — all loneliness is
A clear kind of moveable prophesy, still the
Truth is uniquely common: I'm reconciled to
Create fantasies and to draft a path to them.
Because objects correspond to expectations,
Love, fear can grow from exercise of physical
Retort: the cold and bad breath of a city that
Mold therapeutic thoughts as possibilities
Moil my mind help me hope for better times, which all
Present tense lures. I promise myself a silent
Road that's not cruel, drunks I imagine to be
Roguish, sure sounds (not stealing or soughing my name)
With magic in their distance, a solitary
Train telling a whole story with a whistle through
Singing pines. But, strategically, shrill police
Sirens jar contemplation into a dumb and
Indivisible shock and persuade several
Senses to notice men who crawl or sleep with dogs;
Flaring slashes through haze do hypnotize me. If
Poor eyes wear out, glare remains. Everything simple
Or everything tragic is mutely ever wise
To the disordered weight of interpretation.

Like an accident pushed extremely to the nouns
For deceitful sarcasm, keys slip out of my

Supreme appetite channeled radically for
One more healthy act of coordination; and
Sleep and cold panic cut me down to think short so
That I hardly figure. Fluorescent blasts of
Light that almost burn my flesh sizzle in their own
Electricity. Rarefied by excitement,
My hands squeeze sweat on doughty things; my eyeballs are
Wet with heat. Absurdity can't be calmed! Native
Cognition is wrenched to select the exact key,
Hiding there on fingertips and inspiring me
Insane until I don't choose revelation. But
Over billowy, inaccurate pavement, I've
Madly tripped, lying on icy asphalt breath down
And slowly muttering about inflections of
Stupidity. A clot tore above my eyes, a
Warm flow fills them. God! And I wipe blood on my sleeves
That I might invent patterns in perspective; no
Longer delicate and human, but such a mad
Animal banging around competent insides
Of a paddock. Forever sleeping within a
Lilliputian box-house, the attendant's numb to
Pleasure and change, as he rides unconsciousness to
Limitless freedom. Once more, the key laughs, absconds;
But haranguing contradictions to darkness, the
Physique of Little Car divides dead fate; I howl
Happiness! Consuming the presence of a much
Faded lamp, jangling absolvent pieces of steel,
Which are planned for strong servility, my dull hands,
Trembling as though they would burn away in fire, turn
Every entry: No! I bawl, "Relax or it'll

Disappear.'' Escape whispers that sanity is
Either a matter of control or the only
Positive choice by egotism; my strict view
Cajoles the scintillant angel, my systolic
Nerves jerking as a last chance to aver my first
Innocence nab acquittal! Should the key drop, I'm
Perfectly lost. What you will fight in yourself to
Enjoy something simple! After sensually
Unlocking the absolute door to feel a fond
Cushion's lull of magical fingers, I rebound
Hot ribs bluntly against obstinacy of the
Steering wheel. Invading the ignition, I search;
Low groan low in the motor increases pressure
And dimensions of my hand; rich growling chokes the
Engine. Respire, Material! Respire my own
Desire into your own organs. Machinery
Can pity itself, because it endures flesh's
Ingenuity to extend wide protection
Into accidents and gambles. There's production
To insanity that people find so aptly
Convenient as an independence against
Terror. Instantly, promises enlarge and the
Diminution of form accelerates; therefore,
Cramming at instruments, which control and exalt
Motion, I listen to an interminable
Croak shrink to spurts that condense to a timorous
Disturbance. Warnings too elegiac to be
Mechanical counteract the nothingness of
Oppression and settle the last refuge of our
Being. Nothing. Nothing. Wind counts sweat-frozen lines

On my forehead. Nothing shall gain comparison
With the self-reproaching style of frank moans that are
Machinal and pacifying in a default.
Nothing. Casual patterns will ever deny
The existence of pain by disguising knowledge
In collective treatment. Chance: idle, weighted, yet
Full of every possible consent to every
Human and tender petition and proposal.
Amid the unanswerable answer to a
Whimsical patience, to fragile witness, my hands
Quiver limp and truncate on the wheel. How empty
A man while he is immobile! My eyeballs will
Capricously burn my lids, although what fading,
Conscious forms weaken me dizzy? With dots and spouts
Of colors darting, it seems as though buckets of
Sweat were mixed hungrily with the blood on my face
To boil and purify my redoubtable head.

A precipitate release of tolerance cracks
My face against corporeal, stationary
Intolerance; pain leaks at my disorganized
Cheek, where swollen bones bulge inside a layer of
Crime. Distortions of pleasure, grotesque bodies and
Swallowing atmospheres flush raucously throughout
Involuntary prospects that separation
From prehensive affinity ravishes. If
Reality is conditioned by hope, I can
Never know unqualified pain; if dull with no
Muscle and slumped to nothing, I demur at sleep
Crying for help; and the collapse technically

Is almost complete: I don't recover normal
Directions of my intent or hairless options.

The day's finished: no place to saunter; no one will
Be praised; alienation waits not for pardon
But for simplicity. Surely however time
Reduces the initial seduction of drugs,
Even terror, a profile of blood, bald knots, long
Cuts — all convincingly pledged as sly symbols of
Sovereignity. With nothing else to attempt, then there's
Nothing else to fear. I pry open the cold light;
For consciousness wakes me, flares narcosis, shatters
Panic's time-ruptured concentration; and as though
Stretching off deep sleep, legs and shoulders are wooden
(And if I slow them to life), collect and disperse
Death pains advertising admonitions from the
Body for burglaries by abstraction. I've drooled
My chin and a string of compulsion dangles; parts
Of blood and spit dot my shirt as I squint to set
My origination; a rip in the thigh, gas
Or oil lying rude on my pocket dominate
Nature's foreboding guilt. When respite arranges
My form, sifts for coalescence among fractured
Elements, which float from abortion, decides the
Options night publicizes from syllogistic
Tyranny, involuntary forces become
Escape: I resist the luxuriating and
Congealed inertia, steady the asphalt under
Me, and walk off to find a conscience kindly blessed
By the unknown. My head's bobbing, hurting like a

Worn drunk's; what's left of interminable distance
Churns in immediate sounds I strangely commit
To my intellectual loyalties. Little
Car creaks through terrible cold like a past rattling
Behind me; so that I would extremely know where
They are, details contain my language. Adroitly
Cats can brush across boards like mice in an alley
And tease me mean; I'm in their world, and they scratch as
I'd hit if I could if I weren't human. Missing
Bums, muscleless and without decisions, are yet
Twisted and abstruse and carry my image from
Street to street. What creature died of luxury in
Those with trembling in their veins and alcohol in
Their trembling? Like children, they don't know another
Way or can't transcend themselves; thus only public
Places are home. Moans pronounced slowly in the same
Dialect as those my head aches with insulate
The aggression of space. I am fiercely dumb and
Glassy into glassy stares of a smelly man,
Who says things as vicious as I imagine will
Always save me from the inconvenience of
Lenity. Yes, my guise has broken down here with
Drunks I hate, for I recognize my rare descent
Into Christless hunger, which, to promulgate such
A unique crucifixion, they silhouette; to
Ask anybody for everything, they suffer
Greatly; rigid veins and bones near the skin I've now
Watched carefully, it seems, all my life. Yet, somehow,
Amid the jaded irony of haste and waste,
The old innocents can wait for someone with my

Habits, age, peaceful vanity, fadded physique,
And innovation, and they take their parts from me,
And I'm left looking for someone like my prior Self.

Under the City's higher mist, the safely dead
Lights of a quiescent hotel refuse to be
Their scientific miracle. I remember
A uniformity, bare as brute emptiness,
Ineluctably corroding into wordless,
Masochistic fanaticism: idly sure,
The unsympathetic wood tells the story of
How gladly it used to invite everyone to
Its history but now only those who dislike
References to the future. Big shoes click off,
Nervous voices stuttering suddenly stop, glass
Splintered everywhere splits too easily for my
Steps; commanding their own ponderous dynasty,
Words resent the independence of deduction.
A stray, crippled hound, who gave up home, sniffs as I
Get to the hotel steps, but I don't interest
Him; he hobbles off to search for approximate
Gratifications. Light sprays from a tiny bulb
Freeze the interior unreal, bags of men lie
Over the floor, seasoned heads then stored warm under
Burlap sacks or heavy cardboard will agree with
Simplicity that the cold's also mean. All the
Demands of morning reduce possibilities
As the sign says, "A dollar more upstairs"; better
To accept the lowest station than to forfeit
The last reserve for more immediate pleasure.

What remark satisfies property? Though anger,
Consternation inspire hate from physical things,
Placidity mocks corporeity: wind, stone,
Fire, ice at once attracted and indifferent
To freshest crafts my senses can personalize.
As soon as concrete, underfoot, is uneven,
Something squeals and leaps triumphantly over a
Neutral balustrade; only I meet the rusted
Assumption of a modest doorknob arguing
That promises will exist always alittle
Beneath another well-ordered acceptance of
Decrepitude. Through dark-dimpled wood, a formal
Gash secretly magnifies a performance of
Mythology: the god of antagonism
Is never a match for the god of survival;
For a shivering lump, called (and more correctly
Is again) the insuperable human, will,
Imperative in the cold, defend even the
Charm of defeat. Strong sour clothes, a very old breath
(After I release the static protection of
The door and free a sequence) introduce bodies,
Which, gathered, claim the buried floor and roar at a
Metallic whimper. I begin to step over
People reasonably dead, someone as young as
I replace, another too drunk to know the crime.

It has been told more than once how grief is only
A form of prophecy, how the one faithless tide
That descends into the latest creation of
Sundown reveals the faithful path that the certain

Morning shall follow, how meaning of vatic signs
From greedy famine is reducible to Earth's
Incomplete form, how the use of violence soon
Progresses through a linear equation to
Perfect violence! There is a mad style to the
Universe: irony just as well corrects the
Incorrigible as it stifles powerless
Cries from gentle creatures. License too recalls that
When consciousness is brutal, we regard our strength
As less than physical and, over and over,
Every grief as a historical precedent.

Here hypothesis is not driven by desire.
The rule is also proven: sleep requires no plan
Or conclusion. And, again, generalities
Rest heavily on thoughtless flesh. Memories reach
No terminus, for they exist (soft motions in
A vacuum) — all famously nostalgic thoughts die
For a wish: roamless obscurity, the never
Cold sun nor cancelable moon, the first and last
Episodes of atonement, the passing of good
And old confessions, unchanging superstitions,
Uncompromising liturgy. Since I listen
For common voices, I remember distance shall
Resort to melancholy discovery; our
Past mocks our present where omissions magnify
Ingredients. Faces if general would teach
Joy; childish urges satisfied, wishes defined
By places, idols of parochialism
Verified, and, through mists, recognition rises

So clearly it burns; the truth is distant and close:
The City reflects the unconscious of hamlets.